ALL OF
ANCIENT ROME

THEN AND NOW

BONECHI

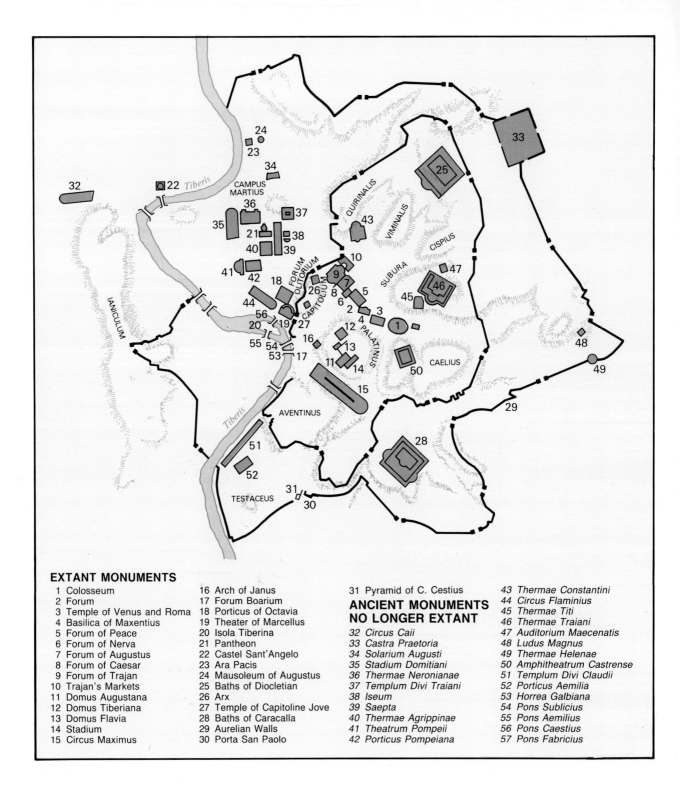

EXTANT MONUMENTS

1 Colosseum
2 Forum
3 Temple of Venus and Roma
4 Basilica of Maxentius
5 Forum of Peace
6 Forum of Nerva
7 Forum of Augustus
8 Forum of Caesar
9 Forum of Trajan
10 Trajan's Markets
11 Domus Augustana
12 Domus Tiberiana
13 Domus Flavia
14 Stadium
15 Circus Maximus

16 Arch of Janus
17 Forum Boarium
18 Porticus of Octavia
19 Theater of Marcellus
20 Isola Tiberina
21 Pantheon
22 Castel Sant'Angelo
23 Ara Pacis
24 Mausoleum of Augustus
25 Baths of Diocletian
26 Arx
27 Temple of Capitoline Jove
28 Baths of Caracalla
29 Aurelian Walls
30 Porta San Paolo

31 Pyramid of C. Cestius

ANCIENT MONUMENTS NO LONGER EXTANT

32 Circus Caii
33 Castra Praetoria
34 Solarium Augusti
35 Stadium Domitiani
36 Thermae Neronianae
37 Templum Divi Traiani
38 Iseum
39 Saepta
40 Thermae Agrippinae
41 Theatrum Pompeii
42 Porticus Pompeiana

43 Thermae Constantini
44 Circus Flaminius
45 Thermae Titi
46 Thermae Traiani
47 Auditorium Maecenatis
48 Ludus Magnus
49 Thermae Helenae
50 Amphitheatrum Castrense
51 Templum Divi Claudii
52 Porticus Aemilia
53 Horrea Galbiana
54 Pons Sublicius
55 Pons Aemilius
56 Pons Caestius
57 Pons Fabricius

© Copyright
CASA EDITRICE BONECHI
Via Cairoli 18/b
50131 Florence — Italy
Fax 055-5000766

Texts by the Editorial Staff of the Casa Editrice Bonechi in
collaboration with: Fabio Boldrini, Stefano Giuntoli.
Cartography: Studio Bellandi - Giovannini - Nariani
Editing: Maurizio Martinelli
Layout: Sonia Gottardo
Translation: Erika Pauli, Studio Comunicare, Florence.
The photographs are the property of the Archives of the
Casa Editrice Bonechi and were taken by
Gaetano Barone, Nicolò Orsi Battaglini, CISCU, Gianni
Dagli Orti, Paolo Giambone, Maurilio Mazzola, Pubbli Aer
Foto, Cesare Tonini.

INTRODUCTION

The traditional date of the foundation of Rome is that given by Varro — 753 B.C. Archaeological studies have however revealed the presence of man here even earlier, with evidence dating as far back as the Bronze age in the second millennium B.C. The first settlement on the site of Rome dates to the early Iron age, at the beginning of the first millennium B.C., with villages of huts on the Palatine and necropolises in the valley of the Forum (along the via Sacra), on the Esquiline and on the Quirinal. These three hills were the first to be inhabited by distinctly separate human groups which to judge from their funerary customs probably also differed in their origin: cremation graves on the Palatine and the Quirinal, inhumation graves on the Esquiline. These settlements must have been very small and independent, if not rivals, as would seem to be indicated by the presence of two separate villages on the Palatine Hill. These communities lived primarily from sheep-herding and had been induced to settle here by the geographical amenities of the site at the crossroads of the most important communication routes by water (Tiber) and land between Etruria, Latium and Campania at the spot where the best ford over the Tiber was located.

The first « Rome » was then nothing but a cluster of small villages of huts whose aspect we can reconstruct precisely from the discovery of their foundations on the Palatine Hill and the hut-shaped cinerary urns found in contemporary necropolises. These huts had their foundations cut into the tufa and they were rectangular in shape with rounded corners, with walls of wattle and daub. Post holes contained the posts which supported the wooden beams of the straw roof and a smoke hole was left in the front part of the roof.

These communities seem to have coalesced into a political, religious federation around the time of the traditional founding date of Rome. The various historical legends relating to the fusion of different peoples, first of all the Latins and the Sabines, into an urban community hark back to this event. Moreover one of the oldest religious festivals, the Septimontium, was based on the participation of the various communities which lived on the hills of Rome and this would seem to indicate that they were distinct from each other.

A particularly important moment in the development of Rome is represented by the reign of Ancus Marcius who augmented trade by exploiting the strategic position of the site. This was the king who built the first wooden bridge over the Tiber, the Pons Sublicius, and who occupied the Janiculum and the Aventine to protect the communication routes that converged on it from the north. In addition Ancus also founded the colony of Ostia at the mouth of the Tiber, a city that was to become Rome's port. But the phase which marks the definitive transformation of Rome from a simple cluster of villages into a real city was the advent of the Etruscan monarchy — the period of the Etruscan kings, Tarquinius Priscus, Servius Tullius, and Tarquinius Superbus, from the end of the 7th century B.C. to all of the 6th century B.C.

3

Literary sources and archaeological evidence reveal that it was at this time that a series of urban structures characteristic of Etruscan culture were undertaken. The wattle and daub huts roofed with straw were replaced by brick houses with tile roofs, the first public buildings were created and real temples took the place of open-air shrines and enclosures. Drainage systems and canals were built to reclaim the swampy land: the Cloaca Maxima drained the valley of the Forum which became the political-commercial heart of the city, while the reclamation of the Murcia valley consented the realization of the first large building for public spectacles, the Circus Maximus.

This intense building activity corresponds to an administrative reorganization which can be traced back to Servius Tullius who created four territorial tribes (Palatine, Esquiline, Collina, Suburana) with political and military functions which replaced the three original aristocratic clans. The army no longer consisted of private individuals with their clientes but was a true citizens army based on a census. The construction of the first city wall of Rome is also attributed to this king and is therefore called « Servian ». Stretches in blocks of cappellaccio have been found under the wall of the 4th century B.C. which follows its perimeter.

Reference has been made to the boom of temple building under the Etruscan kings. The most outstanding included the twin temples dedicated to Fortuna and the Mater Matuta, remains of which have come to light near the Church of S. Omobono, both traditionally ascribed to Servius Tullius. The most important sanctuary built in this period was the Temple of the Capitoline Jupiter, dedicated to the triad of Jupiter, Juno and Minerva, the construction of which was begun by Tarquinius Priscus on the Capitoline, and was finished by Tarquinius Superbus and inaugurated in 509 B.C. by the first consuls of the republic. It is the largest Tuscan temple ever built (65x60 m.) and Vulca, an Etruscan sculptor from Veio, was called in for the decoration.

The Roman republic of the 5th century B.C. was faced with urgent internal problems including struggles between patricians and plebeians and periods of famine and plague, and on the outside, with wars with the Sabines, Etruscans, and the Volsci. In the early years of the 5th century B.C. the ties with the cities of Magna Graecia were strengthened, as demonstrated by the construction in 493 B.C. of the first temple on a Greek plan dedicated on the slopes of the Aventine to Ceres, Liber and Libera and decorated by the Greek artists Damophilus and Gorgasus. But throughout Italy the importance of these fertile cultural and commercial exchanges with Greece diminished in the middle of the century as proved by the sharp drop in importation of Greek vases.

The temples built in this period reflect the problems which afflicted Rome at the time. In 497 B.C. a temple was dedicated to Saturn in view of the god's capacity to protect from the plague; the temple to Ceres, Liber and

What ancient Rome looked like can be seen in the large model begun in 1937 by Italo Gismondi, now in the Museo della Civiltà Romana.

Above: the reconstruction of the Capitoline Hill with, at the center, the large Temple of Jupiter Capitolinus.

Libera is in itself a reflection both of the conflicts that existed between patricians and plebs (the cult is plebeian, and the Aventine is also traditionally a plebeian hill) and of the difficulties the city was facing in procuring sufficient grain because of the dearths (Ceres is the goddess of the harvests). Then in 484 B.C. the Temple of the Dioscuri, gods connected with the equestrian rank, was built and in 433 B.C. the Temple of Apollo in the Campus Martius. In the 4th and 3rd centuries B.C., the phase of cultural contraction was stemmed and Rome once more began to flourish. In 396 B.C. the rival city of Veio was finally vanquished but in 390 B.C. Rome was humiliated by the Gallic invasion. As a result the city walls were rebuilt in 377 B.C. The various stretches still extant show us how large the perimeter of the city was, considering the times. Contacts with Magna Graecia were intensified and the number of artists and craftsmen from there increased in

Rome. The first pottery workshops were set up. Religious buildings were now in stone and on the whole adopted the Tuscan canon. One of the main sanctuaries of this period was Temple C in Largo Argentina. Rome did not yet have a real town plan but the first aqueducts (Aqua Appia) were constructed and some of the important communication routes including the Via Appia (312 B.C.), which led to Capua across the Pontine plain, were realized. In the 2nd-1st century B.C., after the victories in the Punic wars and in the East, Rome had outgrown her role of city-state. The protracted war had led to the ruin of the class of medium and small land owners who formed the backbone of the citizen army, transforming them into an urban proletariat whose rank and file were swollen by the massive immigrations into the capital from the surrounding countryside due to the extension of the large landed estates. On the other hand various large families kept in-

creasing in importance both economically and politically. Urban development clearly mirrors this state of affairs. While on the one hand enormous popular districts with houses of more than one story (insulae) were created, on the other the programs of political propaganda carried out by the most conspicuous members of the community led to the realization of great monumental complexes of a religious or public nature. The building activity in the Campus Martius as well as that in the Forum and the Capitoline is particularly revealing. A series of temples, porticoes and public buildings employing Greek architects and artists were built. These include the Temple of Hercules Musarum (189 B.C.), the Portico of Octavius (168 B.C.), the Portico of Metellus including the temples of Juno Regina and Jupiter Stator, the Porticus Minucia Vetus (107 B.C.), the Theater of Pompey.

Caesar died before succeeding in carrying out his revolutionary town plans, which included the deviation of the Tiber, but with the construction of the Curia and the Basilica Julia he did provide the Roman Forum with its basic plan. Above all he built the Forum of Caesar, and set an example for the policy of tying one's name to the creation of a forum space which continued throughout the period of the Empire.

Caesar's urban policy was taken up, albeit in a less revolutionary way, by Augustus. With the construction of the Forum of Augustus and the Temple of Mars Ultor, the Roman Forum with its series of monuments celebrating the gens Iulia can be considered as completed. Public works of great propagandistic effect were created by the princeps as well as by the members of his circle: the Portico of Octavia with the Greek and Latin libraries, the theaters of Marcellus and of Balbus, the Amphitheater of Taurus, the Pantheon, the Thermae of Agrippa (the first public baths in Rome), the Ara Pacis. A great deal was also done for the maintenance of the extant monuments. In 29 B.C. alone, 82 temples were restored. But Augustus was also responsible for an attempt at providing Rome with a city plan. The city, which already had about half a million inhabitants, was divided into fourteen regions and supplied with other aqueducts such as the Aqua Virgo, and the bed of the Tiber was widened and cleaned of debris.

An event which conditioned the city plan of Rome was the great fire of A.D. 64 in Nero's time. The emperor was thus able to use the area of the districts that had been destroyed for the construction of the Domus Aurea. This sumptuous residence, drawn up as a villa with pavilions, gardens, lakes and groves, occupied a large part of the heart of the city. On the other hand, the reconstruction of entire districts was carried out according to the rational criteria of a real town plan, improving the functionality and safety, with fireproof building material and less crowded dwellings.

The first two emperors of the Flavian dynasty, Vespasian and Titus, inaugurated what was to all effects an anti-Nero building policy. Imposing projects carried out over the Domus Aurea restored the area it occupied to the Roman people. The impressive Flavian Amphitheater (Colosseum) was built on the site of Nero's artificial lake while the Baths of Titus made use of the emperor's private baths. In the same way the works of art which had decorated Nero's residence were exhibited to the public in Vespasian's Forum of Peace. New fires in A.D. 69 and

Left: a bust of the emperor Hadrian (A.D. 111-138). Right: bust of Marcus Aurelius (A.D. 161-180). Both in the Capitoline Museum.

80 forced the Flavian emperors to carry out a great deal of reconstruction.

The Campus Martius was restructured particularly with Domitian, the third emperor of the Flavian dynasty. The Odeon, the Stadium and the Divorum were built. He was also responsible for the Forum Transitorium and, in the Roman Forum, for the Arch of Titus and the Temple of Vespasian and Titus. But the building which best represents his autocratic concept of power is the Domus Augustana, the monumental palace which occupied a large part of the Palatine and which became the imperial residence par excellence.

Under Trajan, the Roman Empire achieved its maximum territorial expansion and the city was provided with imposing monumental and utilitarian works. Trajan's Forum, the largest of the Imperial forums, and Trajan's Markets, an ensemble of storehouses for the capital's supplies, were built.

Hadrian and the emperors of the Antonine dynasty were particularly active in the field of building. This is witnessed by the custom of marking the bricks with the consular dates, a custom which began in A.D. 123. The city was enlarged with the creation of new districts with multi-storied houses. Monumental architecture finds expression in constructions of as imposing size as the Pantheon and the Temple of Venus and Roma.

The age of the Severan emperors was marked by much restoration after the fire under Commodus in A.D. 191, but also by noteworthy creations. The period witnessed the realization of the arch of Septimius Severus, the Septizodium, the Baths of Caracalla and the Temple of Serapis on the Quirinale, one of the largest ever built in Rome. We know exactly what the ground plan of the city was in the Severan period thanks to the Forma Urbis, the monumental marble plan of Rome set up in the Forum of Peace by Septimius Severus.

The 3rd century A.D. represents a period of contraction for Rome, of crises due to the difficult political and military situation. It was no accident that the greatest build-

ing project of the time was Aurelian's city wall (A.D. 270-275) with a perimeter of no less than nineteen kilometers.

With Diocletian and the installation of the tetrarchy, Rome, replaced by four new capitals, was no longer even formally the heart of the Empire. Despite this the city underwent a brief renaissance in building with restorations in the Forum and the Campus Martius after the fire of Carinus in A.D. 283. The greatest complex of thermae in Rome, the Baths of Diocletian, also date to this period. Maxentius made Rome his capital and building activity was brief but intense. In the area of the Roman Forum he built his imposing Basilica and the so-called Temple of the Divus Romulus terminated by Constantine, and restored the Temple of Venus and Roma. On the Via Appia he built his large villa with the adjacent Mausoleum for his son Romulus, and the Circus. Constantine finished various buildings that had already been begun and erected his arch with many reused decorative elements. This is one of the last official monuments to be built in Rome, for after A.D. 330 interest and energy were directed to the new capital Constantinople.

As religious buildings of the new Christian Rome began to rise, from the 5th century on the ancient monuments were abandoned and sacked so the building materials could be reused. In the Middle Ages the most important buildings were occupied and transformed into fortresses by the great families of Rome. This is what happened to the Colisseum with the Frangipane, Trajan's Forum and the Serapeum with the Colonna, the Theater of Marcellus with the Savelli, etc. In addition antique marbles were often reused to decorate churches and new buildings, while that which was considered unusable was transformed into lime in the lime kilns.

The Renaissance, with the intense building activity promoted by popes such as Sixtus IV and Julius II, once more witnessed indiscriminate destruction to clear the ground for new monuments. In addition, this period witnessed the birth of an interest in antiquities and collecting

Opposite: a reconstruction of the Capitoline Hill and the Arx.
Above: the northwestern zone of Rome as it was in ancient times.

that led to excavations and plundering.
Not until the 18th century did things take a turn for the better with the birth of archaeology as a true discipline and with Winckelmann's interest in the history of ancient art. In Rome, from the 19th century to the early 20th century, this led to the excavations and studies by Fea, Nibby, Lanciani, Giacomo Boni. Lastly in the Fascist period enormous damage was caused to the archaeological contexts in the name of the « ideological » recovery of the monuments of Romanism.

9

THE COLOSSEUM

The largest amphitheater ever built in Rome and a symbol for Romanism was the work of the Flavian emperors and was therefore called « *Amphiteatrum Flavium* ». The name Colosseum first came to be used in the Middle Ages and can be traced to the nearby colossal bronze statue of Nero as the sun god which rose up from the site of the vestibule of the Domus Aurea.

The emperor Vespasian began the construction of the Colosseum in the valley between the Caelian, Palatine and Esquiline hills, on the site of the artificial lake around which Nero's royal residence was centered and which had been drained for the purpose. Vespasian's intentions were to restore to the Roman people what Nero had tyrannically deprived them of, as well as that of providing Rome with a large permanent amphitheater in place of the amphitheater of Taurus in the Campus Martius, a contemporary wooden structure erected by Nero after the fire of A.D. 64 but which was no longer large enough.

Works began in the early years of Vespasian's reign and in A.D. 79 the building, which had gone up only to the first two exterior orders with the first three tiers of steps inside, was dedicated. The fourth and fifth tiers were completed by Titus and it was inaugurated in A.D. 80 with imposing spectacles and games which lasted a hundred days. Under Domitian the amphitheater assumed its present aspect and size. According to the sources he arrived « *ad clipea* », in other words he placed the bronze shields which decorated the attic, adding the *maenianum summum*, the third internal order made of wooden tiers. Moreover he also had the subterraneans of the arena built, after which the *naumachie* (naval battles for which the arena had to be flooded) could no longer be held in the Colosseum as the literary sources tell us they once were.

Additional work was carried out by Nerva, Trajan and Antoninus Pius. Alexander Severus restored the building after it had been damaged by a fire caused by lightning in A.D. 217. Further restoration was carried out by Gordian III and later by Decius, after the Colosseum had once more been struck by lightning in A.D. 250. Other works of renovation were necessary after the earthquakes of A.D. 429 and 443. Odoacer had the lower tiers rebuilt, as witnessed by the inscriptions which we can read with

Opposite: the Colosseum as it is now. Above: the Colosseum as it was, as seen in the large model of ancient Rome in the Museo della Civiltà Romana. The section of the amphitheater reproduced to the right is also in the same museum.

the names of the senators dating from between 476 and 483 A.D. The last attempt at restoration was by Theodoric, after which the building was totally abandoned.

In the Middle Ages it became a fortress for the Frangipane and further earthquakes led to the material being used for new constructions. From the 15th century on then it was transformed into a quarry for blocks of travertine until it was consecrated by Pope Benedict XV in the middle of the 18th century.

The building is elliptical in form and measures 188x156 meters at the perimeter and 86x54 meters inside, while it is almost 49 meters high. The external facade is completely of travertine and built in four stories. The three lower stories have 80 arches each, supported on piers and framed by attached three-quarter columns, Doric on the first floor, Ionic on the second and Corinthian on the third. They are crowned by an attic which functions as a fourth story, articulated by Corinthian pilasters set alternately between walls with a square window and an empty space which once contained the gilded shields. The beams which supported the large canopy (*velaria*) to protect the spectators from the sun were fitted into a row of holes be-

Above, and left: the interior of the Colosseum and various passageways.

tween corbels. The canopies were unfurled by a crew of sailors from Misenum.

The arches of the ground floor level were numbered to indicate the entrance to the various tiers of seats in the *cavea*. The four entrances of honor were situated at the ends of the principal axes of the building and were unnumbered, reserved for upper class persons of rank such as magistrates, members of religious colleges, the Vestal Virgins. The entrance on the north side was preceded by a porch (a small two-columned portico) which led to the imperial tribune through a corridor decorated with stuccoes.

The external arcades led to a twin set of circular corridors from which stairs led to the aisles (*vomitoria*) of the *cavea*; the second floor had a similar double ambulatory, and so did the third, but lower than the other two, while two single corridors were set one over the other at the height of the attic.

Above: the interior of the Colosseum with the substructures of the arena at the center. To the side: vaulted passageways leading to the seats.

Inside, the *cavea* was separated from the arena by a podium almost four meters high behind which were the posts of honor. It was horizontally divided into three orders (*maenianum*) separated by walls in masonry (*baltei*). The first two *maeniana* (the second subdivided once more into upper and lower) had marble seats and were vertically articulated by the entrance aisles (*vomitoria*) and stairs. The results were sectors of a circle called *cunei*. It was therefore possible for the seats to be identified by the number of the tier, the cuneo and the seat. The third *maenianum* or *maenianum summum* had wooden tiers and was separated from the *maenianum secundum* below by a high wall. There was a colonnade with a gallery reserved for the women, above which a terrace served for the lower classes who had standing room only.

Access to seats in the *cavea* was based on social class, the higher up the seat the less important the person. The emperor's box was at the south end of the minor axis and

Opposite: two different levels (maeniana) of the grandstands of the Colosseum. Above and at the side: some of the communication corridors leading to the tiers of seats.

In the following two pages: a view of the subterranean structures of the arena (above, left) and details of the mosaics from Tusculum of the 3rd cent. A.D., now in the Museo Borghese, which depict encounters between gladiators (munera) and a hunt (venatio).

this was also where consuls and Vestal Virgins sat. The box at the north extremity was for the prefect of the city (*praefectus Urbis*) together with other magistrates. The tiers closest to the arena were reserved for senators. The inscriptions to be read on some of the extant tiers inform us that they were reserved for specific categories of citizens.

The arena was originally covered with wooden flooring which could be removed as required. In the case of hunts of ferocious animals the spectators in the *cavea* were protected by a metal grating surmounted by elephant tusks and with horizontally placed rotating cylinders so that it was impossible for the wild animals to climb up using their claws.

The area below the arena floor contained all the structures necessary for the presentation of the spectacles: cages for the animals, scenographic devices, storerooms for the gladiators' weapons, machines, etc. They were ar-

SABA[...]S

PVRPVREVS [S]ENTINVS ~ BACCIBVS

ranged in three annular walkways with openings that permitted the areas to be functionally connected with each other. A series of thirty niches in the outer wall was apparently used for elevators which took gladiators and beasts up to the level of the arena. The artificial basin created for the lake of the Domus Aurea was rationally exploited in the construction of the Colosseum, saving an enormous amount of excavation work. Once drained, the foundations were cast and travertine piers were set into a large elliptical concrete platform, forming a framework up to the third floor with radial walls in blocks of tufa and brick set between them. It was thus possible to work on the lower and upper parts at the same time, so that the building was subdivided into four sectors in which four different construction yards were engaged simultaneously. Various types of spectacles were given in the Colosseum: the *munera* or contests between gladiators, the *venationes*, or hunts of wild beasts and the previously cited *naumachie* which were soon transferred elsewheres because of the difficulty of flooding the arena of the amphitheater. Titus' reconstruction of

Above: the model in the Museo della Civiltà Romana with the cross-section of the substructures of the Colosseum with the cells for the wild animals. Below: a terra-cotta plaque from the Roman period showing a hunt in the amphitheater.

18

the naval battle between Corinth and Corcyra in which 3000 men were employed was famous. The gladiator contests took place in the form of a duel between opposing sides, generally until the death of one or the other. In the *venationes* those condemned to various penalties had to fight wild beasts and they were often unarmed. Records of the bloody outcome of these spectacles is to be found in the writings of ancient authors with reference to 10,000 gladiators and 11,000 wild beasts employed by Trajan on the occasion of his triumph over the Dacians or the impressive number of beasts in the hunts organized by Probus for his triumph.

Christians may or may not have been martyrized in the Colosseum. In A.D. 397 Honorius emanated an edict which prohibited gladiatorial games, but they were renewed under Valentinianus III. From A.D. 438 on, only hunts were allowed, which gradually diminished in importance until the last hunt held in A.D. 523 under Theodoric. A final point to consider is the number of spectators the Colosseum was capable of containing: opinions vary but the figure must have been around 50,000.

To the side: the symmetrical arches of the Colosseum. Below: a general view of the Flavian Amphitheater.

Above: the reconstruction of the Baths of Titus near the Colosseum. Left: a stretch of the road paving at the Colosseum. Opposite: the Arch of Constantine.

CONSTANTINE'S ARCH

The largest of the arches erected in Rome is on the route which the triumphal processions took in antiquity, between the Caelian and the Palatine hills. It is 21 meters high, almost 26 meters wide and over 7 meters deep, with three passageways, the central one of which is larger. It was built in A.D. 315 by decree of the Senate and the Roman people to celebrate the 10th anniversary of Constantine's ascent to the throne and his victory over Maxentius in the battle of Ponte Milvio in A.D. 312. The decoration of the arch employed a number of reliefs and sculpture from other monuments. The four detached marble columns on each of the principal sides, surmounted by eight statues of Dacians, are in *pavonazzetto* marble (white with purple veining, from Asia Minor) and date to Trajan's time. Eight tondos about two meters in diameter of Hadrian's period are set in pairs over the side passageways, inserted into porphyry slabs. The presence in some of these medallions of Antinous, Hadrian's favorite, verifies their attribution to this emperor's reign. Four scenes of the hunt (bear, boar, lion and departure for the hunt) are represented, and four sacrificial scenes (to Apollo, Diana, Hercules and Silvanus). The figure of Hadrian appears in each scene, even though his head has

been replaced by that of Constantine in the hunting scenes and by that of Licinius in the sacrificial scenes. At times the nimbus (a sort of halo) used in Constantinian times to confer a sacred character to the figure of the emperor has been added. Stylistically these medallions adhere perfectly to the classical trend of Hadrianic sculpture with a limited number of figures against an almost neutral background and synthetic references to landscape. It is not known where they came from, perhaps from a monument referring to Antinous. On either side of the inscription, which is repeated both on the front and the back of the monument, are eight reliefs from the period of Marcus Aurelius, also set in pairs, which probably came from an honorary arch. They form a cycle which celebrates the return of the emperor in A.D. 173 after his campaigns against the Marcomanni and the Quadi with a series of exemplary episodes which correspond to scenes presented in the Aurelian column.

The first panel shows the departure of the emperor between the Genius (Spirit) of the Senate and the Genius of the Roman People, accompanied by a group of soldiers and his son-in-law Pompey, while the personification of a road invites him to begin his voyage; in the background

Above: the area around the Colosseum and the Arch of Constantine as it once looked. Opposite: various details of the arch.

the Triumphal Gate. The second scene presents Marcus Aurelius as he performs the « *suovetarilis* » sacrifice (a pig, a sheep and a bull) surrounded by attendants and soldiers. In the third the emperor flanked by Pompey harangues the crowd from a tribune. In the fourth panel a barbarian chief is condemned by Marcus Aurelius, while in the fifth he performs an act of leniency towards another barbarian chieftain and his young son. In the sixth panel the emperor receives tribute from a group of barbarians. The seventh panel presents the return of Marcus Aurelius, shown as he is entering the *Porta Triumphalis* accompanied by Mars and Virtus with Mater Matuta and Fortuna in the middle ground and the Temple of Fortuna in the background. Lastly in the eighth panel the emperor, seated at the top of a high podium, is shown distributing donations (*congiaria*) to the people. Behind him the consuls of A.D. 173 and his sons-in-law Pompey and Claudius Severus. A large marble frieze from Trajan's time has also been reused. It has been cut into four parts, two of which are on the short sides of the attic and two on the interior of the central passage. The frieze, of which we have other fragments, was three meters high and over eighteen meters long but the provenance is not known. The scenes represented have to do with Trajan's two Dacian campaigns (A.D. 101-102 and 105-106). From the right we have Roman infantry and horsemen leading Dacian prisoners after the taking of a village, exhibiting the severed heads of the enemy; then comes a charge of Roman cavalry against barbarians who retreat, led by Trajan himself. Finally the entrance of the emperor into Rome accompanied by Virtus while a Victory crowns him. It is interesting to note that the episodes narrated in this historical frieze are very generic without any precise references to the topography or the particular battle as are to be found in Trajan's column, in a spirit interested solely in a triumphant celebration of the imperial victories. Let us now examine

the decorative parts which date to the building of the arch. Beginning with the principal facades of the monument, they comprise the reliefs at the bases of the columns with Victories, Roman soldiers and barbarian prisoners; the keystones of the arches with divinities and allegorical personifications; winged victories with trophies and personifications of the seasons at the sides of the central passageway and river gods flanking the minor openings. On the short sides are medallions with the Sun God and the Goddess of the Moon on a chariot in correspondence to the eight Hadrianic roundels on the main facades. The most important part of Constantine's decoration is however the large historical frieze set above the lesser openings, and which continues on the short sides of the arch. The story begins on the western side with the departure of Constantine from Milan on a chariot preceded by infantry and cavalry. It continues on the south side with the representation of the siege of Verona by Constantine's troops and the emperor protected by two bodyguards while a Victory places a wreath on his head. On the same side is the battle on the Ponte Milvio with Constantine on the bridge accompanied by the personification of Virtus and a Victory, and the defeat of Maxentius and his troops. The short eastern side presents the emperor's entrance into Rome on a chariot preceded by Roman foot soldiers and horsemen. On the north side Constantine makes a speech to the crowd near the Rostra: he is the only person presented frontally according to the hieratic concept of sovereignty which had at this point taken over. The emperor is represented in the same way at the center of the last scene, seated on a high throne in a frontal position, surrounded by his court and personages in togas, while he oversees the distribution of donations to the people at the hands of his officials, which takes place behind him in a high arched portico. In this case too the figures are hieratically represented in different sizes.

Opposite: a view of the model of ancient
Rome with the Roman Forum
at the center. Above: the Forum as it looks
now.

THE ROMAN FORUM

HISTORY

Situated in a valley between the Palatine, the Capitoline
and the Esquiline hills, the area was originally a most in-
hospitable zone, swampy and unhealthy, until surprising-
ly modern reclamation work was carried out by the king
Tarquinius Priscus, who provided the area with a highly
developed drainage system (Cloaca Maxima). Once this
complex reclamation work was finished, the Roman forum became a place for trade and barter. Numerous
shops and a large square known as the market square
were built and a zone was set apart for public ceremonies.
It was here that the magistrates were elected, the traditional religious holidays were kept and those charged
with various crimes were judged by a real court organiza-
tion. After the Punic wars, thanks to the extraordinary
development of the city, the urban fabric of the Forum
took on a new look. As early as the 2nd century B.C.,
various basilicas — Porcia, Sempronia, and Aemilia —
were built, the temples of the Castors and of Concordia
were rebuilt, and the network of roads connecting the Forum to the quarters of the city continued to grow. After
various transformations under the emperor Augustus,
the Roman Forum became so large as to be considered
the secular, religious and commercial center of the city.
After a period in which secular and political interests centered on other parts of the city, the Roman Forum reac-
quired its original prestige under Maxentius and Constantine who ordered the construction of the Temple of
Romulus and the great Basilica of Constantine. With the
decadence of the Roman Empire, the splendid venerable
structures of the Forum were severely damaged by the
Barbarian invasions, especially the Goths (A.D. 410) and
the Vandals (A.D. 455). The Roman Forum meanwhile
became a place of worship for the early Christians who
built the Churches of SS. Sergio e Bacco (on the Via
Sacra), of S. Adriano (on the Curia), SS. Cosma e Dami-
ano (Temple of Peace). As time passed, the Forum was
completely abandoned. What was left of the antique
monuments was used by the people or demolished. During
the Middle Ages the Forum became a pasture for sheep and
cattle (hence its name of Campo Vaccino). For many centuries the prestige of the Roman Forum was a thing of the
past. Not until the early 20th century was there a systematic
re-evaluation of the area with excavation campaigns which
lasted for various decades and which brought back to light
the splendid evidence of the Rome of the kings as well as
that of the republic and the empire.

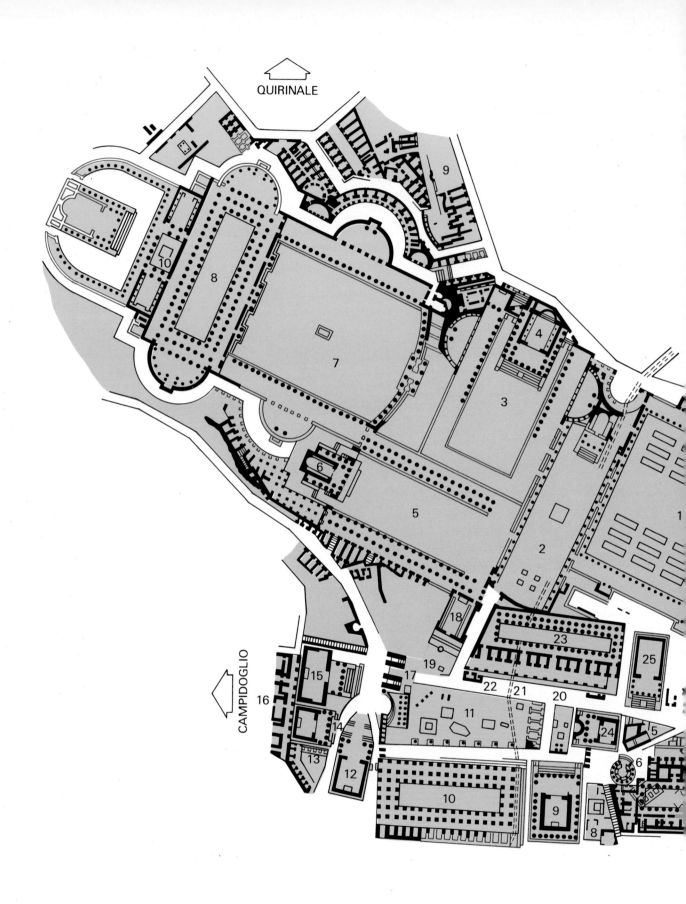

QUIRINALE

CAMPIDOGLIO

IMPERIAL FORUMS

1 Temple of Peace
2 Forum of Nerva
3 Forum of Augustus
4 Temple of Mars Ultor
5 Forum of Caesar
6 Temple of Venus Genitrix
7 Forum of Trajan
8 Basilica Ulpia
9 Trajan's Markets
0 Column of Trajan

ROMAN FORUM

1 Arch of Titus
2 Temple of Venus and Roma
3 Basilica of Maxentius
4 Temple of Divus Romulus
5 Regia
6 Temple of Vesta
7 House of the Vestals
8 Fount of Juturna
9 Temple of Castor and Pollux
10 Basilica Julia
11 Column of Phocas
12 Temple of Saturn
13 Porticus Deorum Consentium
14 Temple of Vespasian and Titus
15 Temple of Concord
16 Tabularium
17 Arch of Septimius Severus
18 Curia
19 Lapis Niger
20 Via Sacra
21 Shrine of Venus Cloacina
22 Temple of Janus
23 Basilica Aemilia
24 Temple of Divus Julius
25 Temple of Antoninus and Faustina

■ Known structures

▨ Structures no longer extant

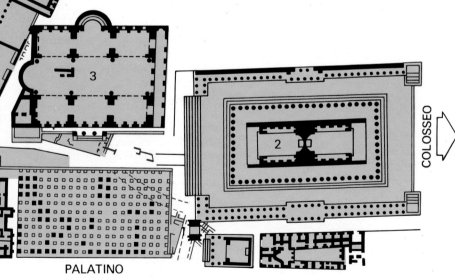

PALATINO

COLOSSEO

27

The eastern side of the Arch of Titus near the Church of Santa Francesca Romana.

1 — THE ARCH OF TITUS

The arch rises in the eastern zone of the forums, south of the Temple of Venus and Roma.

As part of the medieval fortifications of the Frangipane family it survived into the 19th century and in 1822 was restored by Valadier, as recorded in the inscription on the attic on the side facing the Forum. The inscription on the side towards the Colosseum is however contemporary with the arch and tells us that it was dedicated to the emperor Titus probably after his death in A.D. 81 by his brother and successor Domitian to commemorate the victory in the Judaic campaign of A.D. 70.

The arch has a single passageway, and is 5.40 meters high, 13.50 meters wide and 4.75 meters deep, faced with pentelic marble (with piers in travertine restored by Valadier) and on the front and back it has four engaged columns with composite capitals. The decorative sculpture on the outside includes two figures of Victories on globes and with banners above the archivolt, the goddess Roma and the Genius of the Roman People on the keystones and a frieze in very high relief in the architrave with the triumph of Vespasian and Titus over the Jews. Inside the arch, a panel at the center of the coffered vault contains a relief with the apotheosis of Titus, carried to heaven by an eagle, while two large panels with scenes from the Judaic triumph are on either side. The panel on the north depicts a procession in which bearers of the lictor's fasces precede the emperor who is being crowned by a figure of Victory. He is on a quadriga and the horses are led by the goddess Roma (or perhaps Virtus) on foot while personifications of the Roman People (a youth with a bare torso) and the Senate (a man wearing a toga) follow, in a *summa* of the traditional motifs of imperial propaganda.

The panel on the south side presents the procession as it passes through the *porta triumphalis* which is represented in a perspective view; the spoils from the Temple of Jerusalem are carried on litters (*fercula*) and included the seven branched candelabrum, the silver horns, the golden tablet, while various figures bear tablets with handles on which the names of the conquered cities must have been written.

These panels represent a point of departure for a new concept of spatial reality in Roman relief. With respect to the spectator, the figures in the procession no longer move in a horizontal plane but along a convex line that leads to the entrance into the triumphal gate and furnishes an illusionistic sense of depth and movement. The figures are not presented one after the other, but crowd together and are superimposed, represented in differing depths of relief, in an attempt to simulate real space.

The western side of the Arch of Titus.

Opposite: the reconstruction of the Temple of Venus and Roma and, above, what is still visible today.

2 — THE TEMPLE OF VENUS AND ROMA

The temple, set between the Basilica of Maxentius and the Colosseum, stands on a huge artificial platform on substructures which enlarged the hill of Velia. It was superimposed on what remained of the monumental atrium of the Domus Aurea, Nero's regal residence. The gigantic bronze statue (35 m. high) which represented him as Helios was also moved to near the Colosseum.

Begun in A.D. 121 and inaugurated in 135, the Temple of Venus and Roma was designed by Hadrian himself, a « cultured » emperor, passionately fond of art and architecture. The building was set within an enclosing double colonnade which left the two principal facades free and which had two entrance propylaea at the center of the long sides. The dimensions (m. 145x100) of the entire ensemble are imposing.

The temple itself was a large Corinthian decastyle (with ten columns on the front and nineteen on the sides) structure. It lacked the traditional podium of Roman temples but stood on a stylobate with four steps and consisted of two cellae which were set back to back. Entrance to the cellae was via two porches with four columns between the antae. Originally neither cella was apsed and they were covered with flat timber roofs. Their present aspect is the result of restoration effected by Maxentius in A.D. 307, after a fire. The cellae were given apses at the back which contained the cult statues of Venus (in the cella facing the Colosseum) and of the goddess Roma (facing the Forum) while coffered and stuccoed barrel vaults replaced the original ceiling. In addition, the long sides were lined with porphyry columns. Niches meant for statues were framed by small porphyry columns on brackets. The pavement was also renewed in polychrome marble.

The cella of the goddess Roma, facing the Forum, is the better preserved of the two. It is now part of the ex-convent of S. Francesca Romana, and the peristasis has been replaced by a hedge. Only a few of the grey granite columns of the portico are still standing.

In its refusal of the stylistic elements of Roman temple architecture and in turning for inspiration to the Greek world which the emperor fervently admired, this temple, which is one of the largest ever built in Rome, is a perfect example of the classicism which characterizes Hadrian's art. The significance of this veering away from the preceding tradition becomes all the more evident in consideration of the fact that Apollodorus of Damascus, the architect of Trajan's imposing works, criticized the temple on esthetic grounds and paid for his dissention with exile and eventually with his life.

Opposite, above: arches of the Basilica of Maxentius; below:
the reconstruction of the basilica flanked by the Temple of Venus
and Roma. Above: the building as it is today.

3 — THE BASILICA OF MAXENTIUS

Access to the Basilica of Maxentius, which stands outside the current archaeological zone of the Roman Forum, is from the Via dei Fori Imperiali. The building was begun in A.D. 308 by Maxentius and finished by Constantine, who modified the internal layout, shifting the entrance from the east to the south side, on the Via Sacra.

The building stands on a platform which is in part a substructure and which is superimposed on storerooms of considerable size, occupying an area of 100 by 65 meters. The original entrance, which Constantine also retained, opened into a narrow elongated atrium from which three openings led into the large central area, oriented east-west, 80 meters long, 25 meters wide and 35 meters high, covered by three cross vaults supported by eight columns in proconnesian marble, 14.50 meters high, set against piers (none of which are still *in situ*). At the back, right across from Maxentius' entrance, there was a semi-circular apse which contained an enormous acrolithic statue of Constantine (with the uncovered parts of the

body in marble and the rest probably in gilded bronze), the head of which, 2.60 meters high, and a foot, two meters long, were found in 1487.

The aisles on either side of the nave were divided into three communicating bays with transversal coffered and stuccoed barrel vaults. Constantine's new project shifted the axis of the basilica from east-west to north-south, maintaining the tripartite division, with an entrance on the south side with four tall porphyry columns and a flight of steps which led from the Via Sacra to the floor of the building which was partly encased in the Velian hill. Across from this entrance a new semi-circular apse was set into the wall at the center of the north aisle, preceded by two columns and with niches for statues framed by small columns on corbels.

The nave was illuminated by a series of large windows in the clerestory while the side aisles had two tiers of arched windows.

The ground plan and dimensions of the building were inspired by the imposing halls of the imperial baths, which were also called « basilicas ».

4 — TEMPLE OF DIVUS ROMULUS

The building faces onto the Via Sacra between the area occupied by the archaic burial grounds and the Basilica of Maxentius. It appears not to have been a temple dedicated to Romulus, deified son of Maxentius, for the building is of Constantinian date and was probably the Temple to the Penates which we know originally stood in the area occupied at the beginning of the 4th century A.D. by the Basilica of Maxentius and then transferred to an adjacent site. The building is circular in plan and built in brick. The entrance with its original bronze portal opens at the center of the curved facade. It is framed by two porphyry columns with bases in travertine and marble capitals which support a marble architrave. Four niches for statues are on either side the entrance and two elongated apsed rooms flank the temple. They are preceded by two columns in cipolin marble and must have housed the statues of the Penates. In the 6th century A.D. the temple became the atrium of the Church of SS. Cosma and Damian, originally a large room of the Forum of Peace that lay behind it. One hypothesis identifies this temple with that of Jupiter Stator which has never been localized but which was mentioned in literary sources of Constantinian date together with other buildings on the left of the Via Sacra, whereas no mention is made of the Temple of Divus Romulus.

5 — THE REGIA

The building lies on an old tract of the Via Sacra and is surrounded by the Temple of the Divus Julius on the west, the Temple of Vesta and the House of the Vestals on the south, the Temple of Antoninus and Faustina on the north. Ancient sources (Festus, Servius, Plutarch) state that it was built in the period of the kings as the dwelling of Numa Pompilius, second king of Rome according to tradition. In fact the Regia does reveal a complicated alternation of building phases, demonstrated by recent archaeological studies, which go back to the monarchic phase of Roman history.

The site was already occupied in the 8th century B.C. by huts and at the end of the 7th century B.C. the first building was erected in sun-dried brick on a foundation of tufa blocks, with rooms arranged around an unroofed enclosure. It was rebuilt three times during the 6th century B.C. and the arrangement of the rooms around the courtyard was modified. Confirmation of the fact that it was of particular importance, and perhaps the palace of the kings, is provided by the discovery of architectural terracottas and facing slabs which belonged to the third and fourth buildings (respectively 570 and 530 B.C.) and the foot of a bucchero bowl with the inscription « *rex* » dating to the last quarter of the 6th century B.C. This was when the ground plan was radically changed and it be-

Opposite page: the Temple of Divus Romulus. Below: the oldest level of the Regia, brought to light in front of the Temple of Antoninus and Faustina.

came what was then to survive to our time and which remained as it was throughout the republican period. The various remodellings of the second half of the 3rd century B.C. after a fire, in 148 B.C., and in 36 B.C. by the Pontefix Gneus Domizius Calvinus, who also saw to the marble facing of the building, all respect the original irregular ground plan.

The fact that the Regia always maintained its sacred function can be fully appreciated when one considers its historical position. As the seat of the *rex* of the Roman monarchy, the supreme holder of religious as well as political and military power, the Regia became the place in which the *rex sacrorum* of the newly created republic exercised the priestly functions he had inherited from these kings. It is more than chance that the last and final changes in the ground plan of the building date to precisely the years in which the republic was born (traditionally 509 B.C.).

The Regia was the site of extremely ancient cults and rites, with a sanctuary to Mars which had custody of the twelve *ancilia*, the sacred shields used by the ancient college of the Salii for the processions in honor of the god, and the *hastae*, the spears said to vibrate in omen of ruin. There was also a sanctuary of Ops Consiva, the ancient goddess in charge of harvests. For a better understanding of the relationship between these two gods, it helps to recall that originally Mars was connected with the agrestic world, as god of vegetation and the fields and protector of the townsfolk. In his honor, in a ceremony known as *Equos October* that was held at the ides of October, a horse was sacrificed and the tail and genitals were taken to the Regia.

How basically important the Regia was for the religious and civil life of the city is witnessed by the fact that, up to the time of Augustus, this was where the archives of the pontefixes were kept and where the annals and calendar drawn up by the Pontefix Maximus were exhibited. In its final ground plan, preserved from the 6th century B.C., the building has three rooms on the south, the central one serving as an entrance from the Via Sacra for the other two and for the courtyard which lay to the north. The room to the west is the sanctuary of Mars, paved in tufa and with a circular base which may have been an altar, while the room to the east is thought to have been the sanctuary of Ops Consiva. The courtyard is trapezoidal, paved with slabs of tufa, with drainage channels, and with a portico with wooden columns on the north, an entrance to the east and an altar near the west side.

Architecturally the Regia recalls various 7th-century houses of the Etruscan settlement of Acquarossa (near Viterbo) and its relation with the Temple of Vesta and the archaic buildings across the Via Sacra must still be defined, even if it seems likely that originally they formed a single complex.

6 — THE TEMPLE OF VESTA

The temple, which is one of the oldest in Rome, is situated to the south of the Via Sacra in front of the Regia. Its present appearance dates to A.D. 191, when it was re-

stored (the last of many restorations) by Giulia Domna, wife of Septimius Severus. This was where the fire sacred to Vesta, the goddess of the household hearth, had to be kept perennially burning, for disaster threatened if the flame were to go out. This obviously meant the building was frequently in danger of fire.

It seems however that the various reconstructions retained the original orientation with the entrance ritually on the east and the original circular form of the ground plan, which has its prototypes in the huts of the early iron age, according to Ovid in his *Fasti*. The original temple may very well have been a round hut with walls in wood and wattling, plastered with clay, and with a straw roof. The cult of Vesta goes back to the earliest days of Rome. According to tradition the mother of Romulus and Remus was a vestal virgin, and Livy refers that Numa Pompilius founded the order of the vestal priestesses charged with the care of the temple, establishing a retribution paid by the State and particular privileges. Archaeological finds have also verified the antiquity of the temple: when it was excavated, a well in front of it was found to contain votive material from the late 7th century B.C.

As we have said the building is circular and consists of a cella surrounded by twenty Corinthian columns set on a podium 15 meters in diameter faced with marble and with a staircase leading up to it on the east. The roof was conical with an opening for the smoke. The cella, which was articulated externally by engaged columns, contained no cult statue but only the hearth that was sacred to the goddess. A trapezoidal cavity in the podium which can be reached only from the cella may be the « *penus Vestae* » or the *sancta sanctorum* of the temple, a sort of storeroom which only the vestal virgins could enter, which contained the objects Aeneas was said to have brought back after the destruction of Troy, the pledge of the universal glory of Rome. These included the Palladium, an ancient wooden image of Minerva, and the images of the Penates. The temple was closed by Theodosius in A.D. 394.

7 — THE HOUSE OF THE VESTALS

The *Atrium Vestae*, on the south side of the Via Sacra, was a complex consisting of the Temple of Vesta and the house where the vestal virgins lived. As priestesses of the cult of Vesta, they were the custodians of the sacred hearth and were charged with performing the various rites involved. The only feminine body of priests in Rome, the six vestal virgins were chosen among the children of patrician family between six and ten years old. They were required to stay in the order for thirty years, respecting a vow of chastity. Vestal virgins who broke this vow were buried alive in a subterranean chamber outside the Porta Collina, in a place suitably called « Campo Scellerato » (field of iniquity) while their accomplice was condemned to death by flogging in the Comitium. On the other hand they enjoyed important privileges: they were

subtracted from parental authority and the *patria potestas* passed to the Pontefix Maximus, they could travel in the city in a wagon (which was forbidden to women), they had reserved seats at the spectacles and ceremonies and could do as they best saw fit with a sort of stipend they received from the State.

The institution of the vestal virgins is very old and traditionally dates to king Numa Pompilius.

The remains of the *Atrium Vestae* are still visible about a meter below the level of the present building. Of republican date, it is a much smaller structure and, unlike the later one, is oriented north-south. It was joined to the Temple of Vesta by a courtyard, to the south of which was a complex of six rooms (remember that there were six vestal virgins). Part of the mosaic pavement with inserts of irregular marble tiles (*lithostroton*) is still intact.

After the burning of Rome in A.D. 64 the House of the Vestals was rebuilt by Nero in the ground plan it was basically to keep as far as the size and new northwest-southeast orientation, which followed that of the Forum, were concerned. Trajan completely remodeled it and afterwards Septimius Severus restored the entire complex, including the temple. The Vestals left the building in A.D. 394 when the pagan cults were abolished and it was then used for other purposes.

The entrance to the House of the Vestals is to the west, flanked by an aedicula which probably served as a lararium. It leads into a large rectangular central courtyard around which is a colonnade with eighteen columns on the long sides and six on the short sides, arranged in two orders. The courtyard was embellished by three basins, a square one at each end and a larger rectangular one in the center, which was obliterated in Constantinian times by an octagonal brick base for gardening purposes.

The porticoes originally housed the statues which represented the *Virgines Vestales Maximae* (the senior members of the order), many of which have been found in the courtyard together with bases naming them in inscriptions which all date from the time of Septimius Severus on. Some of the statues have been left here, arbitrarily arranged and on pedestals which do not belong to them.

The central part of the east side of the complex is comprised of the so-called « *tablino* », a spacious hall that was originally vaulted, from which six rooms open off. They were also vaulted and are all about the same size (m. 4.15x3.50) which would lead one to think they were the rooms of the six vestal virgins. This group of rooms is

Opposite: two statues of priestesses inside the House of the Vestals. Above: the courtyard of the House of the Vestals with the statues that were originally set under a portico. Right: the reconstruction of the Civil Forum with the Temple of Vesta at the center and the House of the Vestals higher up.

generally thought to be the sanctuary of the Lares and is also where the still extant statue of Numa Pompilius, the founder, may originally have stood.

On the ground floor the south side has a series of service rooms set along a corridor — an oven, a mill, a kitchen, etc. Upstairs are the rooms of the vestals with baths. There must also have been a third floor. The western part of this sector contains an apsed hall, which may have been a remodelling of the shrine erected in the republican period to Aius Locutius. This was the name given to a voice that had come from the grove of Vesta (*Lucus Vestae*) in 390 B.C. warning the Romans of the attack of the Gauls.

A large room, which may have been a triclinium, opens in the west side. Not enough remains of the north side to tell what was there. Remains of the archaic and republican periods are visible underneath. They include the house of the *rex sacrorum* and of the Pontefix Maximus. Caesar, too, lived here when he was Pontefix. An apsed hall used as thermae must also have been connected to this layout.

8 — THE FOUNT OF JUTURNA

Between the Temple of Castor and Pollux and that of Vesta in the area of the Forum there is a spring which must have supplied the archaic settlement of the Palatine; it was identified with Juturna, sister of Turnus, king of the Rutuli (a figure connected with the legend of the origins of Rome), loved by Jupiter who transformed her into a nymph.

A square basin of the republican period, built in *quasi reticolatum* masonry and faced with marble, collected the water. At the center was a base supporting the marble statues of the Dioscuri, placed there to celebrate the mythical episode according to which they were seen watering their horses here after having announced to the Romans the victory over the Latins in the battle of the lake of Regillus (499 B.C.). The statues were found in fragments at the bottom of the basin, on the border of which is to be seen the cast of a stele of the age of Trajan with a relief of the Dioscuri, Juturna, Jupiter and Leda. The aedicula near the basin, with a dedicatory inscription to Juturna, also dates to Trajan. The basin must have been built at the end of the 2nd century B.C. by Metellus and later restored by Tiberius, which coincides with the restoration carried out on the neighboring Temple of Castor and Pollux.

Left: the Fount of Juturna. Below: the columns of the Temple of Castor and Pollux beyond the Basilica Julia.

9 — THE TEMPLE OF CASTOR AND POLLUX

Facing on the square of the Roman Forum to the west of the Arch of Augustus, the temple is separated from the Vicus Tuscus by the east side of the Basilica of Gaius and Lucius.

Tradition connects the founding of the temple to a popular legend in ancient Rome: during the battle of the lake of Regillus in 496 B.C. between Romans and Latins, two unknown young horsemen with a burst of energy led the Romans to victory and immediately thereafter the two were seen in the forum watering their horses at the fountain of Juturna and after announcing the route of the enemy they disappeared in thin air. They were identified as the Dioscuri and in thanks for their aid the dictator Aulus Postumius Albinus vowed to build them a temple. The building was dedicated by his son, *duumvir* in 484 B.C., and completely rebuilt in 117 B.C. by L. Cecilius Metellus Dalmaticus, after his victory over the Dalmations, enlarging the podium.

The temple was once more restored by Verres (governor of Sicily, attacked by Cicero in the *Verrine*) in 73 B.C. The last definitive reconstruction was by Tiberias after the fire of 14 B.C. with a new dedication of A.D. 6.

What remains dates back to this time. The temple was peripteral with eight Corinthian columns on its short sides and eleven on its long sides and with a cella on a concrete base (*opus caementicium*) (m. 50x30x7), originally faced with tufa blocks which were removed in modern times and reused. In the Forma Urbis (marble plan of Rome from the age of Septimius Severus) the building has a central staircase not found by the archaeologists who uncovered two lateral flights of stairs. It may have been eliminated in one of the restorations to make room for the tribune of the Rostra, which, together with the one in front of the Temple of Divus Julius and the Rostras of the Comitia, comprised the « Rostra Tria » mentioned in the sources for the Forum.

The podium we now see dates to the restoration carried out by Metellius in 117 B.C., as do the stretches of black and white mosaic on the floor of the cella.

During the republican period senate meetings were held in the temple and after the middle of the 2nd century B.C. the podium also became a tribune for magistrates and orators in the legislative meetings that took place in this part of the forum square. It was from here that Caesar proposed his agrarian reforms. The building became the headquarters for the office of weights and measures as well and during the period of the Empire part of the treasury of the tax office was kept in rooms in the long sides. Some of these were also bankers' offices.

The cult of the Dioscuri was originally Greek and it was imported into Rome via the cities in Magna Graecia. These twins, sons of Zeus and Leda, were skillful horsemen both in war and in competitions and therefore were the patrons of the Olympic Games and, in Rome, of the

The remains of the columns and the entablature of the Temple of Castor and Pollux.

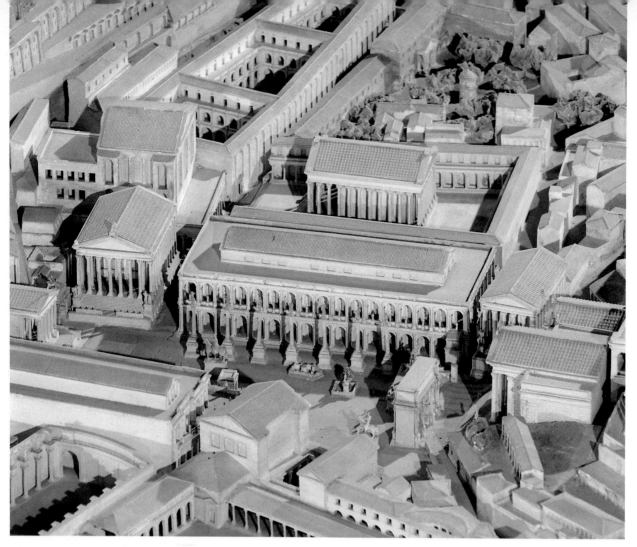

Above: a reconstruction of the Basilica Julia and, opposite, the Basilica as it is now.

Circus games. This is why both in Magna Graecia and in Rome they were the tutelary gods of the equestrian aristocracy. In front of the temple in the Forum, the cavalry corps offered a sacrifice in their honor and passed in review before the censors.

10 — THE BASILICA JULIA

The Basilica comprises the long south side of the Forum and is bordered on the west by the Vicus Iugarius and on the east by the Vicus Tuscus, which separate it respectively from the Temple of Saturn and the Temple of the Castors. Work on the building was begun in 54 B.C. by Julius Caesar, from whom it took its name, and it was dedicated in 46 B.C. The area was previously occupied by the *tabernae veteres* (market shops) and the Basilica Sempronia, built in 169 B.C. by Tiberius Sempronius Gracchus, father of the plebeian tribunes Tiberius and Gaius. At that time the house of Scipio Africanus, as well as various shops, had had to be torn down.

The Basilica Julia was finished by Augustus, who had to reconstruct the building after its destruction in a fire of 14 B.C. In A.D. 12 he dedicated the Basilica to his adopted sons Gaius and Lucius. The fire of Carinus in A.D. 283 caused considerable damage and Diocletian saw to the restoration. It was once more partially destroyed when Alaric sacked Rome in A.D. 410 and it was reconstructed in A.D. 416 by the prefect of the city, Gabinius Vettius Probianus.

The court of the *Centumviri* was held in the Basilica and it also served as a meeting place for those who frequented the Forum. The building, imposing in size (m. 96x48), was composed of a large central space (m. 82x18) with four aisles around it which were meant to serve as corridors. They were vaulted and set on two stories, with arches framed by engaged columns.

The large central hall must have been divided into four parts by wooden partitions or curtains, so that four courts could carry on business at the same time, although in particularly important cases it was used in its entirety. The only part of the building still extant is the stepped podium, while the brick piers are a modern additon.

Still in place are various pedestals for statues, with inscriptions, three of which name Polykleitos, Praxitiles and Timarchus as sculptors. Various « gaming boards »

44

(*tabulae lusoriae*) have been scratched into the pavement and steps, probably by the idlers who hung around the Forum. There are also *graffiti* sketches of some of the statues which seem to have been nearby. Trial digs carried out inside the building have brought to light the remains of the Basilica Sempronia, under which was found the impluvium of what must once have been the house of Scipio Africanus.

11 — THE COLUMN OF PHOCAS

This column was the last monument erected in the Forum. It stands on a stepped brick base and is set in front of the Rostra. The marble Corinthian column is 13.60 meters high and was undoubtedly taken from an older monument. The dedicatory inscription informs us that Smaragdo the esarch of Italy in A.D. 608 set a statue in gilded bronze of the Byzantine emperor Phocas on the top, and sings his praise. Actually Phocas was famous for his cruelty. To begin with he acquired the throne by assassinating his predecessor Mauricius and his children. However he gained particular merit in Rome because in A.D. 608 he presented Pope Boniface IV with the Pantheon which was transformed into a church the following year.

12 — THE TEMPLE OF SATURN

The temple was pseudoperipteral with Ionic columns on a high podium, situated southwest of the Rostra, on the slopes of the Capitoline hill. It was one of the oldest temples in Rome and was erected in 497 B.C. on the site, according to the sources (Festus, Servius), of an altar which had also been dedicated to Saturn and which was then maintained in an area of its own, as revealed by the Forma Urbis (monumental marble plan of the city from the time of Septimius Severus). Some authors say that the foundation of the temple was to be attributed to the last kings, even if the actual building did not take place till the beginning of the republican period with the dedication on the day of the celebration of the Saturnalia, December 17, the Roman end of the year. The building was completely rebuilt in 42 B.C. by the aedile L. Munazius Plancus. The large podium, still extant and entirely faced in travertine, 40 meters long, 22.50 meters wide and 9 meters high, dates to this phase.
As indicated by the inscription on the architrave, the temple was once more restored in A.D. 283 after a fire. The six columns in grey granite on the front, the two in red granite on the sides and the pediment, consisting mostly of reused blocks, belong to this period. A great deal of building material from the structure of 42 B.C. was in fact reemployed. Even the columns do not always pair up with the bases, which vary in style, and with the Ionic capitals. An avant-corps in front of the base consisted of two podia, separated by a flight of stairs which led to the temple. One of these must have contained the headquart-

The Column of Phocas, erected near the Rostra of the Forum.

The remains of the colonnade of the Temple of Saturn, beyond which stretches the Roman Forum.

ers of the Roman State Treasury. The threshold is still to be seen on the side facing the Forum. On the same side a series of regularly arranged holes reveals the presence of a rectangular panel on which the public documents regarding the treasury must have been posted. The cella of the temple contained the statue of the god which was carried in procession for triumphal rites.

When this temple was built, Rome was passing through a particularly critical period due to extensive famines, epidemics and a severe economic and commercial crisis which characterized the years subsequent to the fall of the monarchy. Evidence of the sense of distress which took hold of the Roman people is the erection in these years of a number of temples: to Saturn in 497 B.C.; to Mercury, protector of commerce, in 495 B.C.; to Ceres, goddess of the earth and fertility, in 493 B.C. The building of the Temple to Saturn must also be seen in this light for the god, before being identified with the Greek Cronos, was venerated for a particular characteristic known as « *Lua Saturni* » (the verb *luo* means to loosen, to liberate; *lustrum* means purification), in other words the possibility of freeing the city from its afflictions.

13 — PORTICO OF THE DII CONSENTES

In 1834 a unique structure was brought to light in a raised area near the Tabularium, south of the Temple of Vespasian and Titus. It was comprised of a portico in columns of black cipolin marble (raised in the restorations of 1858) divided into two wings which meet in an obtuse angle, behind which are eight rooms.

Six of the rooms contained pairs of statues in gilded bronze of the twelve Dii Consentes (« counselors » or the highest gods in the Roman pantheon), mentioned by Varro. On the lower floor there are seven rooms that were used as shops. The building as we see it now dates to a Flavian reconstruction, later enlarged in A.D. 367 by the prefect of the city, Vettius Agorius Pretestatus, as indicated in the iscription.

14 — TEMPLE OF VESPASIAN AND TITUS

Set against the east side of the Tabularium, the temple is next to the Temple of Concord on the south and faces onto the west side of the Temple of Saturn.

A mutilated inscription was found on the architrave of the temple which corresponded to the inscription which the Anonymous of Einsiedeln (an 8th-century traveler who visited Rome) noted in its entirey. From it we know that the building is the one the Senate dedicated to the deified Vespasian, after his death in A.D. 79, and thereafter to his son Titus who died two years later. The inscription also tells us of restoration carried out by Septimius Severus and by Caracalla. The temple was built by the emperor Domitian, son of Vespasian and brother of Titus. The whole layout reveals a lack of space, as shown by its proportionately greater width (m. 23x33) and the unique solution of embedding the staircase in the pronaos between the columns. The temple consisted of a cella on a podium with columns along the long walls of the interior. At the back is the plinth on which the cult statues of the two emperors stood. The pronaos consisted of six Corinthian columns on the front and two on the sides, 15.70 m. high, (prostyle temple), three of which at the corner are still standing. Next to the inscription on the architrave were representations of bucrania and sacrificial objects. The podium and the staircase were consolidated by Valadier in 1811.

15 — THE TEMPLE OF CONCORD

Facing onto the square of the Roman Forum, the temple is back to back with the Tabularium, north of the Temple of Vespasian and Titus. One of the first Roman temples built in honor of the personification of an abstract concept, it occupies a particularly important place in the city's civil history. Traditionally it was founded by Marcus Furius Camillus, leader of the aristocratic party, in 367 B.C. to celebrate the pacification between patricians and plebeians as a result of the promulgation of the laws of Licinius-Sextius which granted equal political rights to

both. It was drastically restored and rebuilt in 121 B.C. and newly dedicated to Concord by the patrician consul, Lucius Opimius, after the assassination of Caius Gracchus and his followers. At this time Opimius also founded a basilica which was called after him and which stood near the temple. Between 7 B.C. and A.D. 10 Tiberius completely rebuilt the temple and had it newly inaugurated. The extant remains of the building date to this phase, with a cella that is curiously wider than it is deep (m. 45x25) set on a podium with a central staircase, and preceded by six Corinthian columns which constituted a pronaos which jutted out from the rest of the building like an avant-corps. The only parts still *in situ* are the podium and the threshold of the cella in « portasanta » marble (grey with red veining) on which a cadauces is represented. Fragments of the entablature and a capital decorated with a pair of rams have also been found. During the republic, several famous meetings of the Senate were held in the temple and at one of these Cicero delivered the fourth *Catilinaria*. In the period of the Empire it was also sometimes used for this scope and it was here that the prefect of the praetorium Seianus, accused of plotting against Tiberius, was sentenced to death. With Tiberius the building became a sort of museum with a wealth of Greek sculpture and paintings from the Hellenistic period.

Opposite: a reconstruction of the Forum with (above, from the left) the Temple of Saturn, the Temple of Vespasian and Titus, the Temple of Concord and the Tabularium in the background. Below: a view of the area as it is now.

The Tabularium is at the westernmost end of the Roman Forum, behind the Temple of Concord, the Temple of Vespasian and Titus, and the Portico of the Dii Consentes. The Tabularium was built in 78 B.C. by the consul Q. Lutatius Catulus as part of the reconstruction of the Capitoline after the fire of 83 B.C. and its purpose was that of housing the state archives, whence its name (the « *tabulae* » were the documents).

The building stands on the slopes of the Capitoline on an imposing substructure which compensates for the difference in height between the level of the Forum and that of the valley of the Asylum. It is trapezoidal in plan and has a recess on the southwest side so as to respect the pre-existing Temple of Veiove. The facade facing on the Forum, 73.60 meters long, consists of a row of ten arches framed by Doric engaged columns behind which is a gallery divided into rooms covered with cloister vaults. Originally it had a second story with a porticoed facade of Corinthian columns. Inside the substructure is a long corridor which has six windows that face out on the Forum.

The Tabularium, by the architect Lucius Cornelius, is part of the late republican current of monumental architecture with sub-structures (see the sanctuaries of Tivoli, Terracina and Palestrina) and introduces features which were often to be taken up, such as facades with arches and engaged columns and the cloister vault.

The arch is situated between the Rostra and the Curia and encloses the square of the Roman Forum on the northeast. It was built in A.D. 203 to celebrate Septimius Severus' two Parthian campaigns of 195 and 197.

The arch is about 20 meters high, 25 meters wide and over 11 meters deep and has three passageways, a large one in the center and two smaller ones at the sides with short flights of steps leading up to them. On top is a tall attic with a monumental inscription which dedicates it to Septimius Severus and his son Caracalla. Originally the other son Geta was also mentioned, as can be seen from the holes for the bronze letters (which do not coincide in one point with those there now) which spelled out his name and title. When Caracalla killed him after the death of Septimius Severus, he had his name cancelled from the monuments. Representations of the monument on antique coins show that there was once a bronze quadriga with the emperors on the summit.

The arch is built of travertine and brick faced with marble. On the front are four columns standing on tall plinths decorated with reliefs of Roman soldiers and Parthian prisoners. The decoration includes two Victories, above Genii of the Seasons, which frame the central opening, and personifications of rivers for the side openings, with a small frieze with the triumphal procession of the emperors above. Gods are represented in the keystones: Mars twice for the principal arch and two fe-

Opposite and above. the front and back of the Arch of Septimius Severus.

male figures and two male figures, one of whom is Hercules, on the lesser arches.

But the most interesting part of the decoration is the series of four panels (m. 3.92x4.72) set above the side openings. The story of the two Parthian campaigns unfolds in a series of significant episodes. Each panel should be read from the bottom to the top, beginning with the left-hand panel on the side towards the Forum. Here are represented the phases of the first war, with the departure of the army from an encampment, a battle between Romans and Parthians and the freeing of the city of Nisibis to which the Parthians had laid siege, the flight of their king Vologases, and terminating with a scene of the emperor delivering a speech to his army.

The second panel presents events from the second war: in the lower register the Roman attack on Endessa using war machines, including a large battering ram, and the city opening its gates to surrender; in the central band Abgar, the king of Osrhoene, makes the act of submission to Septimius Severus who harangues the army; in the upper tier is shown an imperial council of war in a *castrum* and the departure for enemy territory.

The third panel shows the attack on Seleucia, a city on the Tigris, with the fleeing Parthians on horseback, the submission of enemies to the emperor, and his entrance into the conquered city.

And lastly the fourth panel shows the siege of the capital, Ctesiphon, with war machines, and the flight from the city of the Parthian king Vologases and, in conclusion, the emperor's speech before the conquered city.

The four panels are fully qualified to be included in the tradition of the Roman historical relief and adapt the composition they inherited from the two spiral relief columns of Trajan and Marcus Aurelius to a different type of monumentality. They are closer to the latter in their narrative scheme, and the representations are more synthetic. Landscape elements and cities are even more schematic, no more than hints of setting, which are however essential in an organic narration of the episodes of war.

A more direct model for these panels was to be found in the triumphal painting which has been lost. In this specific case we know from the sources (the historian Herodotus) that Septimius Severus sent the senate paintings from the Orient which portrayed the events of the Parthian war.

18 — THE CURIA

The building touches on the southwest side of Caesar's Forum of which it is in a sense an adjunct, between the road of the Argiletum and the Comitium.

It represents the seat of the Roman Senate. Tradition attributes the founding of the first permanent Curia to king Tullius Hostilius, from which the name « Curia Hostilia ». It was rebuilt and enlarged in 80 B.C. by Silla but in 52 B.C. it was destroyed in a fire provoked by incidents connected with the funeral of the tribune Clodius. It was then moved from its original site by Caesar who built his Forum there and who began to rebuild the Curia in its present site. His death in 44 B.C. interrupted work and the new Curia, rebaptised by decree of the Senate « Curia Iulia », was not finished until 29 B.C. by Augustus, who also erected a portico known as « Chalcidicum ». After the fire of A.D. 64 it was restored by Domitian in A.D. 94, but it had to be restored once more by Diocletian after the fire of Carinus in A.D. 283 and it was then rededicated in A.D. 303.

The ground plan as we have it now dates to this phase even if Honorius I transformed the building in A.D. 630 into the church of St. Hadrian, and it was frequently remodelled and finally torn down between 1930 and 1936 in order to bring to light the important archaelogical site. The building has a rectangular ground plan with four large buttress piers at the external corners, in line with the facades. The main facade has an entrance door and three large windows which illuminate the hall which is 21 meters high, 27 meters long and 18 meters wide, its proportions respecting the Vitruvian canon for curias. It had a flat timber roof and the present one is obviously modern. Fragments of marble pavement date to Diocletian's time, as does the decoration of the internal walls with niches framed by small columns on corbels and topped by a pediment typical of the taste of the 4th century A.D. (see the facade of Diocletian's Palace in Spalato, the north apse of the Basilica of Maxentius, the Arch of Janus, the Maxentian remodelling of the Temple of Venus and Roma etc.).

The hall has a sector at each long side with tiers of steps on which the chairs of the senators were set. The podium for the president is at the back between two doors and nearby is the base of a statue of Victory which Octavianus had brought from Taranto. At the end of the 4th century A.D., one of the last pagan senators, Aurelius Simmacus, made a last futile attempt to defend the statue and the related « altar of Victory ». But the thesis of his adversary St. Ambrose carried the day and the statue and the altar were removed.

Opposite: a view of the Curia, with the aspect it had in antiquity on the right. Below: one side of the base of the Column of the Decennali depicting the emperor sacrificing velato capite.

Left: the inscribed cippus of the Lapis Niger visible under the paving of the Forum. Opposite: a view of the Via Sacra towards the Arch of Septimius Severus.

18 — THE PLUTEI OF TRAJAN

Two reliefs found in the central area of the Forum in 1872 are to be seen inside the Curia. They are sculptured on both sides and must have belonged to some unknown monument, perhaps the enclosure of the *Ficus Ruminalis* or the Rostra Anziati.

Both panels have a pig, a sheep and a bull, for the « *souvetaurile* » sacrifice, on one side. The other two sides have two historical friezes which refer to moments in Trajan's reign.

One panel commemorates the institution of the *alimenta*: loans which were extended to small land owners, and with the interest used to help orphans study. Assistance was thus furnished both to agriculture and to education. On the left Trajan, escorted by lictors, harangues the crowd from the Rostra Aziaci in front of the Temple of the Divus Julius. Various monuments in the Forum can be recognized in the background: the Arch of Augustus, the Temple of Castor and Pollux and, beyond the Vicus Tuscus, the Basilica Julia, and then the Ficus Ruminalis and the statue of Marsyas. Near the center of the relief, the emperor appears once more on a pedestal, seated and flanked by the personifications of Italia with a child in her arms, perhaps a statue placed in the square of the Forum to celebrate the liberal imperial measures.

The scene on the other panel illustrates the cancelling of the outstanding debts of the citizens: archive officials bring the registers with the outstanding debts and burn them in the presence of the emperor, in the Forum. Spatially and conceptually this scene is a continuation of the preceding relief, as also shown by the buildings on the same side of the Forum represented in the background. From the left are repeated the Ficus Ruminalis and the statue of Marsyas, then the rest of the eastern side of the Basilica Julia, the Vicus Iugarius, the Temple of Saturn, the Temple of Vespasian and Titus, to end up with the Rostra Anziati. What we have here is a typical example of Roman narrative art which represents episodes which happen at different times, together, in an ideal unity of time, by means of a careful topographic unity into which the episodes are set.

19 — THE LAPIS NIGER

This is the only surviving monument of the ancient Comitium, set in the northwest corner of the Forum near the Curia, after Caesar and Augustus reorganized the area. It was discovered in 1899 by Giacomo Boni in the course of the excavations of the Roman Forum.

It consists of an area approximately square paved in black marble and separated from the travertine pavement of Augustan times by a balustrade of marble slabs. A religious complex dating to the archaic period was found under this pavement. It consisted of a « U » shaped altar of two superposed cushions (only the lower one has been preserved), a base in the form of a truncated cone, probably for a statue, and a pyramidal cippus or stele with a *boustrophedon* inscription (to be read alternately from top to bottom and from bottom to top) in archaic Latin, partially destroyed and not completely comprehensible even today.

Evidently what we have here is the *lex sacra* of the sanctuary. A curse for those who defiled the holy place has been identified and the king (« *Recei* ») and the *calator* (« *Kalatorem* »*)* are mentioned. It is the oldest known monumental inscription in Latin and dates to the second quarter of the 6th century B.C. The entire cult complex belongs to the 6th century B.C., as confirmed by the votive pottery, some of which was Greek, and the bronze statues found here. From this it can be deduced that when the *rex* is named, it really refers to the Rome of the kings and not the republican *rex sacrorum*, a priest who inherited the king's religious functions. In this respect the mention of the *calator*, or herald, also makes sense for it was in the Comitium where the sanctuary is situated that the king convoked the archaic assembly of the Roman people as well as carrying out the necessary ritual sacrifices.

This cult site is known to us from Roman literary tradition (especially through Festus) as ill-omened for it was connected with the death of Romulus, as well as the tomb of Faustulus or of Hostus Hostilius, grandfather of the king Tullus Hostilius. On the whole it is now thought to be the Volcanal, the archaic sanctuary of Vulcan, where Romulus was killed by the senators according to a tradition which is echoed in Plutarch's « *Life of Romulus* ». Dionysius of Halicarnassus in describing the Volcanal defined it as an open-air sanctuary and mentions an iscription in « archaic Greek letters » of the type appearing in the Greco-Chalcidian alphabet used to write the archaic Latin inscription on our stele. There is in any case no doubt as to the connection of this site with the functions of the Comitium; it may represent the *heroon*, the funeral monument of the founder of the city (as in the *agorai* of the Greek cities), patron of the ancient asemblies of the Roman people, the « *comitia curiata* ». The black marble pavement however seems to date to the late republican period, in commemoration of the disastrous profanation of the site during the Gaulic invasion of 390 B.C.

Above and opposite: two stretches of the Via Sacra.

20 — THE VIA SACRA

Various ancient sources have provided detailed information on the Via Sacra but the entire route followed by this course, which changed along with the history of the city of Rome, has not yet been completely identified. There are various hypotheses regarding the use of the term « Sacra ». Varro tells us it depended on the fact that it was the route taken by the sacred processions while Festus adds the mythical episode of the sacred pact between Romulus and Titus Tatius which tradition locates here. In any case it seems likely that a decisive element in the acquisition of the name is the fact that the oldest and most important places of worship were situated along this route. As far as the route is concerned, the sources inform us that, according to the sacerdotal terms, the Via Sacra was to go from the Arx on the Capitoline to the Shrine of Strenia near the Colosseum, crossing the Forum by way of the Regia and the House of the *rex sacrorum*. This last brief stretch was the one the people knew best. It then passed in front of the Basilica Aemilia, the Regia and the Temple of the Divus Romulus, then probably veered left between the Temple and the Basilica of Maxentius in the direction of the Carinae; the road that led from the Temple of the Divus Romulus towards the Arch of Titus may also at a later point in time have been called Via Sacra.

After Nero's fire of A.D. 64 the route followed by the Via was notably modified. The street level was raised and the road was straightened out towards the site of the bronze colossus of the emperor. Stretches of two lower layers of the cobble paving of the republican period have also come to light. The Via Sacra was further modified by Hadrian after the construction of the Temple of Venus and Roma.

21 — SHRINE OF VENUS CLOACINA

A round marble base in front of the Basilica Aemilia was part of a shrine comprised of an open - air enclosure. The goddess worshipped here was Cloacina, who was charged with purifying the waters of the Cloaca Maximus which entered the area of the Forum at this spot. This goddess was later identified with Venus who inherited the name as one of her epithets as well as the attributes. As attested by the sources, the cult statues of Venus and of Cloacina were to be found in this shrine. According to the mythical history of Rome this is also traditionally the place where Virginia was killed by her father in his attempt to preserve her from the lust of the tyrannical *decemvirus* Appius Claudius.

22 — TEMPLE OF JANUS

The temple lay near the Basilica Aemilia, across the road of the Argiletum where it entered the Forum. No trace of the building has remained but Nero's coins tell us what it looked like. It consisted of a double arch, the doors of which stayed open in times of war and were closed in times of peace. Inside was the double-headed statue of Janus, ancient god in charge of entrance-ways and of all beginnings.

Above: the little that remains of the Basilica Aemilia between the Curia and the Temple of Antoninus and Faustina. Opposite, above: the reconstruction of the basilica and, below, remains of the structures and the reliefs.

23 — THE BASILICA AEMILIA

It comprises the long side of the square of the Roman Forum and is fronted to the west by the road of the Argiletum.

This is the only basilica of the republican period still extant. The others were the Sempronia, the Opimia and the Porcia. It was founded in 179 B.C. by the censors M. Fulvius Nobiliores and M. Emilius Lepidus after whom it was originally called Basilica Aemilia et Fulvia. Various changes were made throughout the centuries by the *gens Aemilia*. Marcus Aemilius Lepidus, consul in 78 B.C., decorated the architrave of the lower story with a series of gilded shields bearing the portraits of his ancestors and also took pains to restore it as witnessed by an image of the basilica on a coin and the inscription « *M. Lepidus Aimilia ref(ecta)* ».

In 55 B.C. the *edile curule* L. Emilius Paolus (brother of the triumvirate Lepidus) began a thorough restructuration which was finished, with a contribution from Caesar, by his son L. Emilius Lepidus Paolus in 34 B.C., the year of his consulate. In this phase the basilica acquired its basic ground plan and was superimposed on the *tabernae novae* which lay in front, just as the Basilica Iulia had

been superimposed on the *tabernae veteres*, to constitute the long sides of the Forum square in line with Caesar's project. In 14 B.C. it was destroyed by fire and was rebuilt by L. Emilius Lepidus Paolus himself and by Augustus. The decoration of the portico and the cella date to this time. It was finally rebuilt one last time after the fire of A.D. 410 during the invasion of Alaric's Goths as witnessed by the coins of the beginning of the 5th century found fused on the pavement of this period.

The basilica is probably of eastern Hellenistic origin and in Rome served to house the political, economic and judiciary functions of the Forum when the weather made it impossible for them to be carried on outside.

The Basilica Aemilia consisted of a large hall (m. 70x29) divided into aisles by rows of columns. The nave, about twelve meters wide, was flanked by one aisle on the south and two aisles on the north. There are remains of paving in colored marble. On the side towards the square of the Forum, the building was preceded by a two-story portico with sixteen arches on piers. The three columns still standing belong to the reconstruction after A.D. 410. Behind the portico was a series of *tabernae* for bankers, built to take the place of the *tabernae novae*, wiped out in the construction of the basilica. The three entrances that led to the hall were set between them.

Above: the remains of the Basilica Aemilia.

Fragments of slabs in pentelic marble which belonged to a figured frieze that ran along the architrave of the first interior order have been found in the basilica. The subject matter was concerned with stories relating to the origins of Rome: the childhood of Romulus and Remus with Acca Larenzia, the founding of the city, the rape of the Sabines, the killing of Tarpeas and others. They probably date to the restoration of 78 B.C., as indicated by similar representations of the same episodes from the cycle of Roman legends on coins of the same date.

24 — THE TEMPLE OF DIVUS JULIUS

The temple is at the eastern end of the Piazza del Foro with the Basilica Aemilia to the north, the Temple of the Castors to the south and the Regia to the east.
It was built in 29 B.C. by Augustus as part of his project for the restructuring of the area of the Roman Forum, in the intent of giving the square a new disposition. This building closed off the square on its short east side and thus excluded once and for all the archaic monuments

Opposite: the base of the Temple of Divus Julius with the Altar of Caesar. Above: the reconstruction of the temple, to be identified at the center of the Forum.

such as the Regia and the Temple of Vesta.

The temple is dedicated to the deified Julius Caesar (it is the first example in Rome) and stands on the site where his body was cremated after it had been brought near the Regia, his official residence as Pontefix Maximus. A marble column was erected here in memory of the « father of the country », as stated in the inscription, replaced by a semicircular exedra with an altar, which opens at the center of the temple podium, on the facade. The Temple of Divus Julius, of which only the base is still extant, consisted of a cella on a podium, access to which was provided by a flight of stairs on either side. The pronaos had six Corinthian columns on the front and two at the sides and, except for the facade, it was surrounded by a colonnade, to be identified as the *Porticus Iulia*. The rosters taken from the ships of Antony and Cleopatra in the battle of Actium in 31 B.C. seem not, as formerly believed, to have decorated the podium, but were on the front of an orator's tribune which stood before the temple. The building is connected to the Basilica Aemilia by the portico dedicated to Gaius and Lucius, Augustus' grandsons, and to the Temple of the Castors (the brothers Tiberius and Drusus) by the Augustan arch of the victory of Actium, which was replaced in 19 B.C. by the one of the « Parthian » victory. It therefore belongs to a real propagandistic program in which the emperor's aim was to have the whole square echo with the name of the *gens Iulia*.

61

Opposite: the Temple of Antoninus and Faustina. Above: a detail of the colonnade and the entablature.

25 — THE TEMPLE OF ANTONINUS AND FAUSTINA

The temple faces onto the Via Sacra, in front of the north side of the Regia to the east of the Basilica Aemilia.

The monumental inscription on the architrave, still extant, identifies this building as the temple to the emperor Antoninus Pius and his wife Faustina. It was originally erected in honor of Faustina alone, by her husband, after her death in A.D. 141. Then in A.D. 161 when Antoninus Pius also died, a Senate decree dedicated the temple to the deified imperial couple.

There are two reasons why the building has reached us in good condition; first because the Church of S. Lorenzo in Miranda was built inside in the early Middle Ages, and secondly because it was unusually solidly built. Oblique grooves in the upper part of the columns into which ropes to pull them down were to be fitted show that attempts to tear down the pronaos so as to reuse the marble were to no avail.

The temple, imposing in its size, consists of a cella built in blocks of *peperino*, originally faced with cipolin marble, and placed on a podium, access to which is by a modern staircase, with a brick altar in the center. The pronaos consists of six Corinthian columns on the front and two on each side, in cipolin marble and seventeen meters high, on some of which images of gods are engraved. The frieze has confronting griffins and plant designs.

Interesting fragments of sculpture, which belonged to the cult statues of the imperial couple, have been found near the temple.

Opposite: an all-over view of the Forum and the Imperial Forums rebuilt. Above: a detail of the Imperial Forums as they were two thousand years ago.

THE IMPERIAL FORUMS

HISTORY

Although the Imperial Forums were built near the precedent Forum of republican times, the underlying concept was more rational and grand. These enormous public squares (80-90,000 sq. meters) were enclosed by porticoes and an equestrian statue of the emperor was often to be found at the center while the square was shut off at the back by an imposing temple.

The Imperial Forums were created with the scope of enhancing the prestige of the city and providing the citizens with a place for their markets, from which they could listen to harangues, and where they could participate in religious ceremonies. The first forum built was the **Forum Iulium** (54-56 B.C.), under the auspices of Caesar

himself. Next came the **Forum of Augustus** (31-32 B.C.), the **Forum of Vespasian** or of Peace (71-75), **Nerva's Forum** (A.D. 98) and lastly **Trajan's Forum** (113). After the 6th century, the Forums were completely neglected and began gradually to be destroyed. During the Middle Ages a tiny portion was recuperated and a small district came into being which blended with the other Roman ruins. Most of it however became a mud-field and was rebaptized the zone of the « Pantani » or bogs, and the splendid buildings of Imperial times were destroyed or gravely damaged. Forgotten for centuries, the area was partially urbanized in the Renaissance but not until the 19th century and above all the 20th were the remains of this once magnificent architecture brought to light and the Via dei Fori Imperiali created.

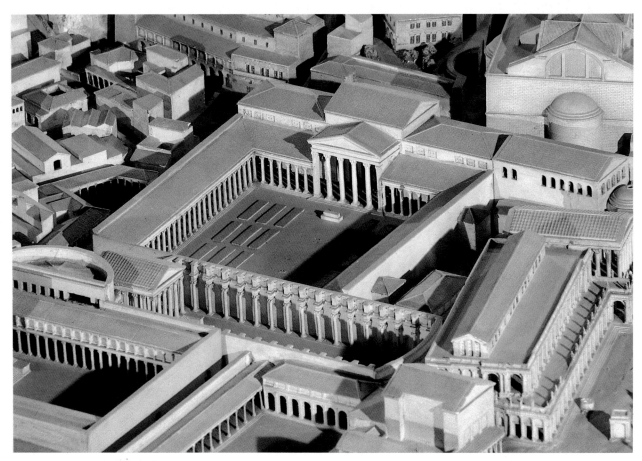

The reconstruction of the Temple of Peace.

1 — THE TEMPLE OF PEACE

The Temple of Peace closed off the Imperial Forums on the southeast. The old route of the Argiletum separated it from the Forum of Augustus to which it was later joined by its inclusion in Nerva's Forum.

The structure was built by the emperor Vespasian on the site of the old *Macellum*, the covered public market, around A.D. 74 to celebrate the victory of the Judaic campaign and the return of peace. It was destroyed by fire in A.D. 192 in the time of Commodus and was restored by Septimius Severus.

The complex, later known as « Forum of Peace », consisted of a large square with gardens, enclosed on three sides by porticoes. Those at the sides, each have a rectangular exedra preceded by two columns, while at the back there was a real temple with an apsed hall which contained the cult statue. The front had a projecting pronaos with six columns which were taller than those of the portico. In front was a rectangular altar.

Two of the halls which were adjacent to the temple have in part been preserved. In one of them, which was quite large (m. 34x18x18), the holes in the wall were for the ele-

ments which supported the eleven rows of marble slabs comprising the *Forma Urbis*, a monumental plan of the city which measured 235 square meters, set here by Septimius Severus. Only fragments have survived but even so the plan is an incomparable source of information on the topography of ancient Rome. In the 6th century the hall on the other side of this wall was transformed into the Church of SS. Cosmas and Damian. It must originally have been used as a library to judge from the niches in the walls which were meant to contain the volumes.

In addition to the Greek and Latin Libraries, the Temple of Peace housed a real museum of Greek art including statues by Polykleitos, Phidias, Leochares, Myron, paintings by Nicomacus, Helen, etc., taken in part from Nero's Domus Aurea and placed there by Vespasian, as well as the instruments from the Temple of Jerusalem, brought to Rome by Titus in A.D. 70.

Nothing else besides these two halls remains of the complex except a column in African marble, a fragment of an architrave and one of the exedrae of the portico situated under the Torre dei Conti.

The plan of the Temple of Peace and the presence of gardens hark back to eastern Hellenistic models.

2 — THE FORUM TRANSITORIUM
AND THE TEMPLE OF MINERVA

The **Forum Transitorium** takes its name from the fact that it lies between the republican Roman Forum, the Forum of Augustus, the Forum of Caesar, and Vespasian's Temple (or Forum) of Peace.

It was built by Domitian and inaugurated by Nerva (which is why it is also called Nerva's Forum) and was meant to unify the various forum areas of Rome. It is superposed on a stretch of the old road of the Argiletum and the long narrow shape (m. 120x45) was dictated by the limited space available, which also explains the absence of an internal portico and the illusionistic device of setting up a row of columns a short distance from the outer wall. Above them was an attic with reliefs illustrating myths connected with Minerva and a frieze with scenes of feminine occupations. On the south side a stretch of the outer wall in blocks of *peperino* and two Corinthian columns, the so-called « Colonnacce », are still standing. In the frieze is the myth of Arachne and on the attic a figure of Minerva.

The short entrance side was curved, while the pronaos of the **Temple of Minerva**, a Corinthian hexastyle on a podium with a tripartite apsed cella, projected from the back. Drawings from the 16th century show us that at that time the temple was still standing and the dedicatory inscription mentioning Nerva could still be deciphered on the architrave.

In 1606 Pope Paul V had it torn down so he could use the building materials and the decorations in the Aqua Paola Fountain erected on the Janiculum.

Right: a section of the portico of the Forum Transitorium with the so-called « Colonnacce ». Below: remains of the structures in the Forum of Nerva.

3-4 — THE FORUM OF AUGUSTUS AND THE TEMPLE OF MARS ULTOR

The **Forum of Augustus** lies between the Forum of Caesar on the west and the *Subura* district to the east. It was later enclosed on the north by the Forum of Trajan and to the south by the Forum Transitorium.

The Forum of Augustus was constructed after costly expropriations on the part of the emperor so that he could free the area which was occupied by private dwellings. He had vowed a temple to Mars Ultor (the avenger) before the battle of Philippi of 42 B.C. in which Brutus and Cassius had died, to commemorate the avenging of the death of Caesar, his adoptive father. It was not until forty years later in 2 B.C. that the project was finished and the great square (m. 125x118) could be inaugurated. On its long sides the square has colonnades and on the short southeast side it ends in the mass of the temple.

Two large symmetrical semi-circular exedrae were set into the wall behind the porticoes, at the height of the temple, and a bronze quadriga with the emperor was placed at the center of the square.

The entrance side, to the southwest, adjacent to the eastern side of Caesar's forum, is now under the Via dei Fori Imperiali as is the case with the front part of the square and the colonnades. There were also two secondary entrances at the back of the forum, near the large

wall in *peperino* and *pietra sperone* (lithoid tufa), thirty-three meters high, which isolated the complex from the *Subura* district. One was an entrance with three openings to the north, the other was the so-called « Arco dei Pantani » to the south, with one opening which led via two flights of stairs to the arches on either side of the Temple of Mars Ultor, dedicated to Drusus Minor and Germanicus. The porticoes on the long sides have Corinthian columns in cipolin marble and were decorated at the top by caryatids and shields bearing the heads of divinities. It is uncertain whether they had two floors or were topped by an attic. Behind the colonnade, on the back wall of the porticoes and on the walls of the two exedrae there were a row of niches for statues, framed by engaged columns, also in cipolin marble, which supported a marble entablature. The name and offices of the personages represented were inscribed on the base of each statue, while a slab under the niche contained the *elogium* with the various deeds. At the center of the north exedra was the statue of Aeneas, flanked by smaller statues of Anchises, Ascanius, the Julii and the kings of Alba Longa. Similarly, the statue of Romulus was set at the center of the south exedra, where he was surrounded by the *Summi Viri*, the eminent personages in the history of republican Rome, which then continued along the walls of both the porticoes. A large hall richly decorated in marble opened off the back to the portico on the north side. The room contained two paintings by Apelles and a colossal statue of Augustus (14 m. high), set here by the emperor Claudius.

Augustan propaganda intent on demonstrating that the mythical traditions and the republican history of Rome converged in the person of the emperor is exemplified here. Aeneas is the ancestor of the city but he is also the ancestor of the *gens Iulia*, and through Iulo, of the kings of Alba Longa. The correspondence between the series of statues of illustrious persons in Roman history and Virgil's list of the glorious predecessors of Augustus to be found in Book VI of the *Aeneid*, obviously with the same ideologic intent, is also significant.

The **Temple of Mars Ultor** consisted of a cella on a tall podium faced in marble, access to which was via a staircase with an altar at the center and two fountains at its outer edges. It had eight Corinthian columns over seventeen meters high on the front and eight on the long sides, while the back was without (*peripteros sine postico*). The inside also had seven columns in two rows along the walls and, at the back, an apse with the cult statues of Venus, Mars and the Divus Iulius. It pays to remember that the first two were the divine parents respectively of Aeneas and of Romulus, who as we have seen are also represented in the exedrae as a means of strengthening the concept of the glorification of the *gens Iulia* which lies at the basis of the entire Forum of Augustus.

Right: a statue of Augustus placed in the Imperial Forums in modern times. Opposite: the remains of the Temple of Mars Ultor in the Forum of Augustus and, below, a reconstruction of the structures.

69

5-6 — THE FORUM OF CAESAR
AND THE TEMPLE OF VENUS

This **Forum**, the first of the great imperial forums, lies northeast of the republican Roman Forum, along the Clivus Argentarius. Caesar had to spend enormous sums of money (sixty million sestercians according to Cicero, one hundred million according to Svetonius) simply in acquiring the land and in expropriating the private buildings that occupied the area. Not even the fact that the Rostra had to be moved and the old Curia Hostilis had to be demolished deterred Caesar from carrying out this ambitious project, which it must be remembered was private.

The project was planned as an elongated esplanade, 160x75 meters, with porticoes on three sides, and, in the back, the large Temple of Venus Genetrix which Caesar had vowed before the battle of Pharsalus against Pompey in 48 B.C.. The Forum was planned in 54 B.C. and dedicated in 46 B.C., but work was finished by Octavianus. Reconstruction of the temple and of the porticoes, with the construction of the Basilica Argentaria, was undertaken by Trajan, and a new inauguration of the whole was held in A.D. 113. Lastly Diocletian had it restored after the fire of A.D. 283.
The Temple of Venus Genetrix and about half of the square in front and the portico on the west have been ar-

chaeologically studied. A series of shops from Caesar's period have been brought to light. They vary in size and were built in tufa or travertine on three floors, vaulted under Trajan, and with a double colonnade in front. There was a statue of Caesar on horseback at the center of the square.

The **Temple of Venus Genetrix** had a single cella on a high podium with a flight of stairs on each side. There were eight Corinthian columns on the front and nine at the sides, in line with the formula of the *peripteros sine postico*. Two square fountains were set in front of the podium. The interior walls of the cella were articulated by six columns on each side. In the back was an apse with the cult statue of Venus Genetrix but the cella also contained other works of art such as paintings by Timomachus of Byzantium. The temple decoration as we know it now dates to Trajan's period.

The Forum of Caesar is a great example of personal propaganda paid for by the dictator, who at the time was a consul, out of his own pocket, in the intent of enlarging the republican forum which no longer sufficed. This also explains the importance placed on the cult of Venus Genetrix who, as the mother of Aeneas, was also considered the first ancestor of the *gens Iulia*, to which Caesar belonged.

In its layout the complex recalls oriental models with its typical stylistic features of axiality and frontality in line with the absolutist tendencies the dictator was beginning to develop and it was to be the model for the later Imperial Forums.

Opposite: section of the colonnades of the Forum of Caesar. Below: the reconstruction of the Forum of Caesar and the Temple of Venus with, on the right, the larger Forum of Trajan.

7-8 — TRAJAN'S FORUM AND THE BASILICA ULPIA

Trajan's Forum extends northwards from Caesar's Forum and is oriented in the same direction. It is at right angles to the Forum of Augustus with which it borders on the west. The last and most imposing of the Imperial Forums in Rome, it is the most important public work carried out by the emperor Trajan and his architect Apollodorus of Damascus. In order to build the forum, the ridge between the Capitoline Hill and the Quirinal had to be eliminated. This imposing complex (300 m. long and 185 m. wide) was built between A.D. 106 and 113, financed by the proceeds of the Dacian war that had just been concluded.

The curved entrance side was situated in an open space between the Forum of Augustus and that of Caesar. At the center was a triumphal arch with a single passageway, known to us only from representations on coins, articulated on the front by six columns which framed statue-filled niches, over which were tympanums with *imagines clipeatae* (portraits set inside shields); Trajan in a triumphal chariot pulled by six horses, trophies and other statues were set on the high attic.

The arch led into an enormous square (m. 118x89) with columned porticoes on the two long sides. It was closed at the back by the Basilica Ulpia placed orthogonally. At the center of the square there was a large statue of Trajan on horseback. The porticoes had an attic on which were set statues of Dacian prisoners, framing shields with portraits. Behind the colonnades, on the long sides, were two imposing semicircular exedrae preceded by six piers. The discovery here of fragments of large-scale portraits of Nerva and Agrippa (Nero's mother) reveal that Trajan had continued the gallery of his illustrious predecessors which Augustus had already realized in the porticoes and exedrae of his Forum.

Practically none of the layout of the square is visible for it lies under the Via dei Fori Imperiali. What we have are the eastern exedra and the ground level of the portico on the same side, with the bases of the columns still *in situ*.

The **Basilica Ulpia**, which closed off the back of the square, has also been excavated only in part. This is the largest basilica ever built in Rome, 17 meters long and almost 60 meters wide, taking its name from the family name of the emperor. Entrances were on the southeast long side: a central entrance with three openings, and two side entrances, with a single opening each, framed by columns and topped by groups of statues, as can be seen on coins. The interior of the Basilica had a monumental central area, separated by imposing granite columns from the four side aisles which surrounded it on all four sides. These were separated from each other by smaller columns in cipolin marble. Two large hemicycle exedrae, set on the same axis as those of the square, opened off the short sides.

The Forma Urbis of the Severan period shows us that Trajan had located the Atrium Libertatis in the southwestern exedra. This was where all the ceremonies and proceedings for the liberation of slaves took place, in precedence taken care of in a building that was torn down

Opposite: a statue of Trajan set in the Imperial Forums in modern times. Above: remains of the colonnade of the Forum of Trajan in front of Trajan's Markets.

in the construction of the Forum.

Statues of Dacian prisoners and fragments of sculpture and a frieze with figures of Victories killing a bull and decorating a candelabrum with garlands were found in the area of the basilica.

Two openings on the northwest side of the basilica led to a courtyard where Trajan's column still stands, flanked by the two libraries which according to the sources contained the emperor's private archives and a collection of praetorial departmental orders. The library to the southwest has been brought to light under the Via dei Fori Imperiali. It is a rectangular room with niches in the walls, raised on three steps and framed by columns in two orders, in which the closets which contained the volumes were set. On the back wall is a larger niche with marble architectural decoration which must have housed the statue of a god. The spiral frieze on the column could be contemplated from the upper floors of the libraries.

The **Temple of the Divus Trajanus** and of the Diva Plotina terminates the Forum to the northeast. It was built in A.D. 121 by Hadrian after Trajan's death. Not much is known about this temple which stood on the present site of the Church of S. Maria di Loreto and which must have been of colossal size with eight Corinthian columns on the front and eight on each side, over 20 meters high.

The general concept of Trajan's Forum is derived from the neighboring Forum of Augustus, but many innovations have been introduced. One of these is the position of the Basilica Ulpia, set transversely so that it closed off the back of the square which would normally be occupied by a temple set frontally.

But the most important aspect of the layout is its clear analogy to that of the *castra*, or military encampments. In fact each *castrum* had a main square (*principia*) on which the tents of the commander and the tribunes opened and where the troops were harangued, closed on a short side by a basilica. Beyond this were the military archives, to which the two libraries in the forum correspond. And lastly the column is in the spot where the sanctuary of the *vexilla*, the insignia of the legion, were generally placed.

This then is a program which recalls the military vocation of the emperor, to whose conquests Rome owed the moment of greatest territorial expansion in its history.

Opposite and above: Trajan's Markets as they are and as they were in antiquity.

9 — TRAJAN'S MARKETS

The construction of Trajan's Forum required the removal of part of the Quirinal hill and the architect, Appollodorus of Damascus (who built the Forum as well), brilliantly made use of the slopes to realize a unified structural complex which we call Trajan's Markets.

The front of the markets consists of a large hemicycle in brick behind the eastern exedra of Trajan's Forum, echoing its shape and separated from it by a road paved with large irregular polygonal blocks of lava which had been polished. A series of *tabernae* open in the bottom floors with doorways with jambs and lintel in travertine, over which are arches framed by brick pilasters with bases and capitals in travertine, supporting small pediments. These arched windows provide light for the corridor on the upper floor onto which another row of shops set against the rock of the cut on the hillside face. On the ground floor, at the sides of the tabernae, are two large semi-circular halls, with windows and covered by half domes, that may have been used for schools.

The third level of the complex is a road that rises steeply and which was called « Via Biberatica » in the Middle Ages, a name which may indicate what the shops there were used for (*biber* = drink or *piper* = spices). Most of the *tabernae* on the side towards the Forum have been

destroyed, while those uphill are still well preserved.

A staircase leads from the Via Biberatica to a great basilical hall covered with six cross vaults springing from travertine corbels. Two floors on the long sides house various rooms: on the lower floor six shops open off on each side with doorways with surrounds in travertine, while on the upper floor, reached via internal stairs, a series of *tabernae* opens onto a corridor that faces onto the central hall.

On the south side of the basilica this fifth level leads to a series of rooms on two floors (with an overall total of six stories) which includes an apsed room that must have been the main office for the direction and supervision of the entire complex.

Trajan's Markets were probably a sort of wholesale storehouse for the distribution of essential commodities, such as grain, oil and wine, managed by the state through imperial personnel who supplied the *negotiatores* of the provinces. Retail sales must also have taken place here at « political » prices below the market price, as well as, on occasion, the distribution of the dole to the people (*congiari*) by the emperor. The Markets represent an important moment in Trajan's commitment to seeking rational solutions for the problems of the Roman food policy.

From an architectural point of view they are a real masterpiece of town planning by Apollodorus of Damas-

Above: Trajan's Column. Opposite, two parts of Trajan's Markets dominated by the Torre delle Milizie *(above) and the Loggia of the Knights of Rhodes (below).*

cus, who, as the occasion demanded, freely adopted functional solutions for the best possible use of the space he had at his disposition, in a spirit that was in a sense at the other pole of that involved in the realization of the adjacent Forum of Trajan, based on the principle of axiality and symmetry that the political representational aspect of its function required.

10 — TRAJAN'S COLUMN

The column stands in Trajan's Forum, between the two libraries, behind the Basilica Ulpia and in front of the Temple of Divus Trajanus. Dedicated in A.D. 113, it is Doric and « *centenaria* », that is 100 Roman feet high (29.77 m.), composed of 18 drums of luna marble. It stands on a high cubic base with four eagles holding garlands at the corners and low relief trophies of stacks of Dacian weapons on three sides. Altogether it is almost 40 meters high, and at the top there was a statue of Trajan which was lost and, replaced by one of St. Peter by

Pope Sixtus V in 1587.

The entrance door to the monument is on its main side facing the Basilica Ulpia. Set above it is an inscription on a panel supported by two Victories which celebrates the offering of the column to the emperor by the Senate and the Roman people as an indication of the height of the hill before it was cut down to make way for the new Forum. Actually the column was meant to serve as the tomb of the emperor and the entrance in the base leads to an antechamber and then a large room which contained a golden urn with Trajan's ashes. The same door on the right leads to a spiral staircase of 185 steps, cut in the marble, which rises to the top of the column.

A continuous frieze, like an unrolled *volumen*, moves around the shaft of the column. About 200 meters long and varying in height from 90 to 125 centimeters, it represents Trajan's two victorious Dacian compaigns of A.D. 101-102 and 105-106, separated in the narration by a figure of Victory writing on a shield. All the phases of the two wars are minutely described with precise geographical and topographical details. The battle scenes alternate with representations of the transferral of troops,

the construction of encampments, bridges, roads, of speeches made to the troops, sieges, the deportation of the conquered enemy etc. The documentary and didactic purpose is evident from a ceaseless search for items of information meant to help the spectator understand the events more clearly.

There are over 2500 figures in the frieze and Trajan appears about 60 times. Originally the relief was colored, but now the painting can only partially be seen. There may also have been painted inscriptions with the names of the places where the action took place. The work is attributed to the so-called « Master of the Feats of Trajan », perhaps Apollodorus of Damascus, the architect of the Forum.

Left, above: the Via Biberatica inside Trajan's Markets, with a view of the hemicycle below.

Below and opposite: two details of the casts of Trajan's Column in the Museo della Civiltà Romana: they depict the legionaries bringing the emperor the heads of the conquered enemies (below), the Roman troops, with a « testudo »', besiege a city (opposite, above) and the chief of the Dacian prisoners brought into the emperor's presence (opposite, below).

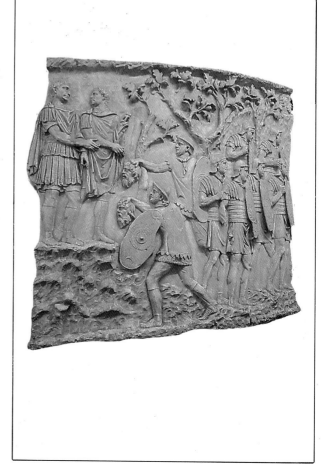

Above: a general view of the reconstructed Palatine. Opposite: the eastern part of the hill.

THE PALATINE

HISTORY

This is the most famous of Rome's hills and it retains the earliest memories of the old city. In fact the first groups of huts of the square city were built on the Palatine, before they spread over to the adjacent hills. Important public buildings, large temples and many private dwellings such as those of Cicero, Crassus and Tiberius Gracus went up here. Later the hill became the residence of the emperors of Rome who had their sumptuous palaces built here, including the **Domus Augustana**, the **Domus Flavia**, the **Domus Transitorio**, the **Domus Aurea**, and the **Domus Tiberiana**, of which considerable remains are still extant. The Palatine was then the residence of the Gothic kings and of many popes and emperors of the Western Empire; in the Middle Ages convents and churches were built. Finally in the 16th century most of the hill was occupied by the immense structures of **Villa Farnese** and the **Orti Farnesiani** (the first real botanical gardens). Archaeological excavation was begun in the 18th century and evidence of Rome's past was brought to light, including remnants of the **Domus Augustana**, the splendid paintings of republican period and the remains of the first dwellings that stood on the hill, as well as the imposing 16th-century entrance portal to the Orti Farnesiani.

Ruins of the supporting brick structures on the east side of the Palatine hill.

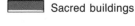

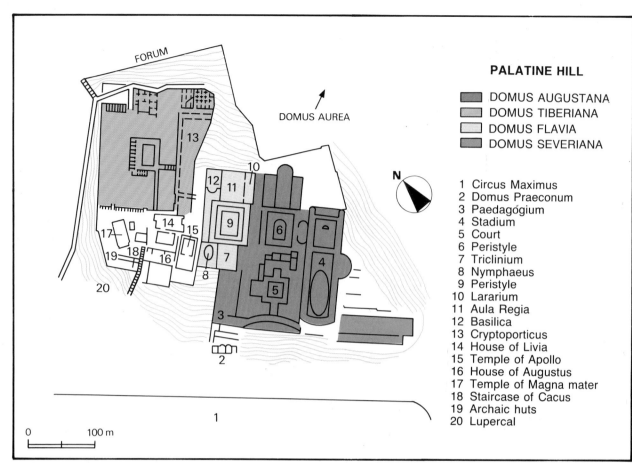

PALATINE HILL

- DOMUS AUGUSTANA
- DOMUS TIBERIANA
- DOMUS FLAVIA
- DOMUS SEVERIANA

1 Circus Maximus
2 Domus Praeconum
3 Paedagógium
4 Stadium
5 Court
6 Peristyle
7 Triclinium
8 Nymphaeus
9 Peristyle
10 Lararium
11 Aula Regia
12 Basilica
13 Cryptoporticus
14 House of Livia
15 Temple of Apollo
16 House of Augustus
17 Temple of Magna mater
18 Staircase of Cacus
19 Archaic huts
20 Lupercal

FORUM

DOMUS AUREA

0   100 m

Opposite: the present eastern entrance to the remains of the Palatine. Above: the Stadium of the Domus Augustana.

THE DOMUS AUGUSTANA

When Domitian's large palace was built on the Palatine the disposition of the hill and its role as the site of imperial residences were firmly established. The building went up between the beginning of Domitian's reign and A.D. 92, with some parts, such as the stadium, finished later. It was used as the emperor's palace up to the end of the Empire. The complex is divided into three parts: the Domus Flavia which was used for purposes of state, the Domus Augustana, a private wing, and finally the Stadium, or large garden in the shape of a circus.

The core of the Domus Flavia was the large peristyle with an octagonal fountain at the center. All that is left of the portico today are the bases of the columns. A series of large rooms surrounded the courtyard. On the north side was the so-called « Aula Regia » with two entrances framing an apse. The walls of this imposing hall were articulated by niches containing statues flanked by tall columns. From the apse at the center back, on the room's main axis, Domitian granted official audience and received the homage of his subjects in a spirit that was quite in keeping with his self-asserted divinity (he was the first emperor who had himself called « god »).

Two large rooms, the Basilica and the so-called « Larari-um », one on either side, communicated with the Aula Regia. The Basilica is a rectangular hall which terminates in an apse and is divided into three aisles by two rows of columns. Its structure would seem to indicate its use at some kind of public ceremony which required the presence of the emperor for whom the apse was reserved. The function of the Lararium is more problematical for the name seems to be purely conventional and does not actually indicate the sanctuary of the Lares.

The Triclinium with its colonnaded front opens on the south side of the peristyle. This imposing room, which terminates in an apse at the back and has columns on the walls, was the emperor's luxurious dining room. At the sides, clearly visible through large windows, were two large nymphaea with oval fountains of which only one is still extant.

Two earlier dwellings have been brought to light under the Domus Flavia. From the decoration on the walls they have been called the « House of the Griffins » (late 2nd cent. B.C.) and the « Aula Isiaca » (circa 20 B.C.).

The Domus Augustana, by which the entire complex was originally meant, represents the emperor's private apartments. It spreads out over two levels, following the lay of the artificial levelling of the hill. The southern part which is on the ground floor opens onto the Circus Maximus

This page and opposite: the remains of the Domus Augustana set around the Stadium.

with a curvilinear facade. A vestibule with two semicircular rooms at the sides leads to a large peristyle with a monumental fountain with ornamental *pelta* motifs in the center, surrounded by rooms on two stories. Flights of stairs lead to the upper level (the same as the Domus Flavia) with interconnecting rooms which lead into a second peristyle with a small temple on a small island at the center of a large basin. There may have been a third peristyle to the north in an area that has been very poorly preserved, while on the east is a large elliptical room with a double internal colonnade, parallel to the stadium.

The eastern sector of the complex was comprised of the so-called Stadium, a large garden in the form of a circus measuring 160x50 meters with the back set against the curve of the Circus Maximus. A portico on two floors ran all around it while in the center it had a « *spina* » of which only the semi-circular extremities remain. The east has an exedra-shaped tribune at the center.

The Domus Aurea represents an important moment in Roman architecture. Domitian's architect Rabirius here created the canonic formula of the dynastic residence, effecting a synthesis between structural functionalism — with the division into official and private sectors — and baroque decoratism with a mixture of curved and straight lines in the ground plan and attention paid to the illusionistic aspects and perspective effects, which were already present in the Domus Aurea.

Above: the remains of the Domus Flavia. Left: the nymphaeum of the Domus Flavia.

Above: the remains of the Domus Flavia.

THE DOMUS TIBERIANA

The House of Tiberius was the first of the imperial palaces to be conceived organically as a palace and the first to be built on the Palatine. It rose behind the Temple of the Magna Mater on the western slope of the hill which overlooks the Roman Forum. Only a small part of the building has been excavated, for the area it occupied was turned into the Orti Farnesiani in the 16th century.

Still visible on the south side of the complex is a series of rectangular rooms, constructed in brick and with barrel vaults which may have been built by Nero. The vaults preserve traces of pictorial decoration with scenes and figures set in panels that can be dated to the third century A.D. In the south corner of this side of the building is an oval basin with steps, which seems to have been a fish pond.

The eastern side consists of a long cryptoporticus with more painting and mosaic pavements. At the north end, a section branches off to the west. It was built later to connect the complex to the Domus Augustana.

The north side of the Domus Tiberiana overlooks the Roman Forum and is the best preserved part. It consists of two groups of rooms oriented diversely which flank an old road, the Clivus Victoriae. The easternmost sector, with rooms oriented like the rest of the building, is a reconstruction of Domitian's time after the palace had been gutted by the fires of A.D. 64 and 80. Adjacent rooms with oblique ground plans also extend beyond the Clivus Victoriae, passing over it with large arches. These can be attributed to Hadrian.

A part of the central part of the building was excavated in the second half of the 19th century and then covered over again. A vast peristyle, with various rooms opening off it, came to light. It was connected to the cryptoporticus on the east side via two corridors.

THE DOMUS AUREA

In the early years of his reign Nero had the Domus Transitoria built as his personal residence. As indicated by the name, house of passage, its purpose was to join the imperial property on the Palatine and Esquiline hills. After the fire of A.D. 64 had destroyed most of it, the emperor began the imposing complex which was to replace it and which was called Domus Aurea (« house of gold »), the name itself an indication of the magnificence with which it was conceived.

The complex occupied an area of about 100 hectares and stretched from the Palatine to the Esquiline, the Caelian and the Oppio, after numerous public and private buildings destroyed in the fire had been expropriated. The Domus Aurea was designed by the architects Severus and Celerus and decorated by the painter Fabullus, as well as being embellished with a great number of statues pillaged from Greece.

Literary sources (Svetonius) tell us it was built like a villa, sumptuously articulated into pavilions separated from each other by large luxuriant groves, full of animals, both wild and domestic, with gardens, fountains, and ornamental waterworks. The entire complex was centered around a large artificial lake (« like an ocean » says Svetonius) which lay in the valley where the Colosseum was later to rise. A colossal bronze statue (over thirty meters high) stood in the vestibule and represented Nero as the sun god.

The architects had invented all sorts of extravagant refinements for the emperor's pleasure; the ceilings of the banquet halls were made of mobile ivory plaques so that flowers and perfume could be showered down on the guests; the most important of these halls was round and rotated with the movement of the earth. The baths were supplied with ocean water and sulphurous water. But what particularly offended public opinion of the time was the enormous extension of a layout that was the living quarters for a single individual, even if he was the emperor, and the fact that it rose in the heart of the city, occupying a large part. Significant is the following famous epigram: « Rome has become a single house; emigrate to Veio, Quiriti, unless this house also ends up by occupying Veio ».

All that remains of the entire complex of the Domus Aurea (Otho, Vespasian and Titus lived in various parts) is a pavilion on the Oppian hill, 300x90 meters, for it was encased in the foundations of Trajan's Baths after it had been destroyed by fire in A.D. 104. This sector consists of two architecturally distinct parts. The inorganic irregular ground plan of the rooms where these two parts meet is proof of the fact that they were built at different times.

The guiding principles for the construction of the western part were axiality and orthogonality, with a perfect orientation based on the cardinal points. To the south is a vast rectangular courtyard with a fountain at the center, surrounded by porticoes on three sides and a cryptoporticus on the north which also served to support the hill on top. A series of rooms was arranged all around. On the west various intercommunicating rooms overlook the courtyard. To the east is a nymphaeum, comprised of a large rectangular room with a four-columned porch on the side facing the courtyard and one at the back. This leads to a smaller room (the real nymphaeum) that is vaulted and with windows looking out on the courtyard. At the back wall there was a waterfall and the water was collected in a basin at the center.

The walls of the nymphaeum were decorated with a mosaic that was removed in antiquity, framed by a band of shells. Part of the decoration of the vault (10.20 m. high) still exists, with medallions that were originally done in mosaic, one in each corner and an octagonal one in the center, set against a sienna yellow background. The mosaic can still be seen in the central medallion alone, in which Ulysses is shown offering a cup of wine to Polyphemos.

The more important rooms were on the south side of the large rectangular courtyard. A double room in the center divided the ensemble into two distinct sets of identical apartments. On the east and west were two alcoved rooms which were probably bedrooms (« cubicula ») for the emperor and his wife. They were connected to two smaller rooms which faced on the courtyard, at the sides of which were two apsed rooms.

Only a small part of the pictorial decoration of these rooms has survived but it suffices to give us an idea of the splendor of the whole and the high level achieved by the painter whom tradition has identified as Fabullus. Some of these rooms take their names from the painting. The Room of the Owl's Vault was once the large central hall, the Room of the Black Vault is the alcove of the room to the east, and the Room of the Yellow Vault is the contiguous room. The apsed room to the east also still has remnants of decoration.

These paintings, rediscovered in the 15th century, were the source of inspiration for a group of Renaissance artists who created a decorative genre which went by the name of « grottesques » from the name « grotte » given to the rooms of the Domus Aurea where they scratched their names on the stucco. In particular Raphael and his circle used this new style in the decoration of the Vatican loggia.

Communication with the eastern sector of the complex, as said before, takes place with brusk architectural solutions which do nothing to fuse the two distinct architectural units into one. The ground plan is more articulated, with two centers of attraction consisting of a polygonal courtyard and a vast octagonal hall.

A large room known as the Room of the Gilded Vault because of the gilded stucco decoration opens off the center of the north side of the courtyard. It is oriented north-south like the rooms that surround it. The series of rooms to the east of this chamber lead to a cryptoporticus which, like the one on the western side, served as a buttress for the hillside. Above this was a canal which brought water to an apsed rectangular nymphaeum which led to the « octagonal hall », a piece of daringly innovative architecture, with a passage from the octagonal shape of the room to a spherical dome without the use of pendentives, and with large doors on each side which lead to the rooms that radiate around it. Two of these, which are obliquely set with regards to the nymphaeum, have cross vaults and rectangular exedrae set into the walls.

Part of the pictorial decoration has also been preserved in the eastern group. The stuccoes of the vault and apse can still be seen in one of them, as well as a picture of Achilles and the daughters of Lycomedes.

The two sectors of the Domus Aurea also differ stylistically as far as painting is concerned. The eastern part falls into the Pompeiian Style IV, based on complex perspective views, superposed planes, architectural fantasies, while the Style III paintings found in the western sector tend more to a decorative miniature type of painting, with small panels that stand out against uniform backgrounds, as if they were suspended in delicate floral ornaments. It therefore seems obvious that the two complexes belong to different chronological periods. One hypothesis identifies the western part of the rooms as part of the Domus Transitoria, and the eastern part as the Domus Aurea.

The remains give us no more than a partial idea of what Nero's imposing project was like. The fine marble and anything valuable it contained were already removed in antiquity. We can only try to imagine the sophisticated baroque illusions and perspective views which lay at the core of Nero's concept, for it was afterwards used as a substructure for Trajan's Baths.

Above: the reconstruction of the Palatine and the Circus Maximus. Below: a reconstructed model with cross sections of one of the huts on the Palatine dating to the early Iron age.

89

Left: a relief of the Imperial age depicting a race inside the Circus Maximus.

THE CIRCUS MAXIMUS

The largest building for spectacles in Rome stood between the Palatine and Aventine hills, in the Murcia valley. The sources (Livy, Dionysius of Halicarnassus, etc.) tell us that this was where the king Tarquinius Priscus had the first circus for chariot races (initiated by Romulus) built, assigning boxes to senators and knights.

Now only the lay of the land, much higher than the original arena, betrays the form of the original structure. For a long time it was built entirely of wood. In 329 B.C. the *carceres* or stalls for the horses and chariots were built in painted wood, as well as the *spina* in the center which covered and channeled the stream which ran through the valley and around which the race was run.

In 196 B.C. Stertinius erected a triumphal arch at the center of the curving south side, while in 174 B.C. the censors Fulvius Flaccus and Postumius Albinus had the *carceres* built in masonry and placed seven stone eggs along the *spina* as markers for the number of circuits the chariots had run. In 33 B.C. Agrippa had bronze dol-

Opposite: the Circus Maximus as it is now and, above, a reconstruction showing what it originally looked like.

phins set up for the same scope. Caesar also used the Circus for hunts. On the side towards the Palatine, Augustus had the *pulvinar*, a sacred box reserved for the tutelary gods of the games, set up and in 10 B.C. he had the obelisk of Ramsetes II taken at Heliopolis placed on the spina. The obelisk, 23.70 meters high, was transferred to Piazza del Popolo by Pope Sixtus V in 1587. In Augustus' time the Circus Maximus had three orders of tiers for spectators of which only the lower one was in masonry and the other two were in wood.

Claudius took a hand in the restoration after a fire in A.D. 36. He had the *carceres* rebuilt in marble and had the *metae* (the goals, conical extremes of the *spina*) covered in gilded bronze. The Circus was once more destroyed in the fire of A.D. 64. Nero rebuilt it and increased the number of posts. In A.D. 81 an arch in honor of Titus took the place of the one of Stertinius on the short south side. Another fire under Domitian ravaged the building and reconstruction was finished by Trajan. Caracalla enlarged the Circus. Under Antoninus Pius and Diocletian the *cavea* collapsed twice and there were numerous victims. Constantine restored it and Constantius II embellished the *spina* with a second obelisk of

Tuthmosis II, which came from Thebes and was even higher than the other one (32.50 m.), and which Pope Sixtus V had placed in Piazza San Giovanni in Laterano in 1587.

The Circus measured 600x200 meters and had a capacity of 320,000 spectators who watched the chariot races that were held there. The most important were those of the *Ludi Romani* the first week of September, which opened with a religious procession in which the highest religious and civil authorities of the city took part.

The Circus Maximus appears on coins from the time of Trajan, Philippus etc. and in mosaics in Piazza Armerina and Barcelona. In Barcelona the *spina* and all the monuments that decorated it are represented and the shrines and aediculae for the gods.

Not much of what is left of the building which was excavated in the 30s on the curved side towards the Palatine can be seen. There are radial walls which supported the upper tiers of seats and vaulted rooms with staircases from Trajan's period. A few shops have been brought to light under the Church of S. Anastasia on the slopes of the Palatine, separated by a road from a larger room of undetermined use.

MAMERTINE PRISONS

Under the Church of S. Giuseppe dei Falegnami, on the slopes of the Capitoline hill, north of the Temple of Concord, are the « prisons » known later in medieval times as « Mamertine ». Only a part has been preserved. It corresponds to what the sources call the « Tullianum » from the traditional attribution to Servius Tullius.

The travertine facade of the building conceals an earlier one in tufa and can be dated from the inscription referring to the consuls Gaius Vibius Rufinus and Marcus Cocceius Nerva who were in office between A.D. 39 and 42. A modern entrance leads into a trapezoidal chamber built in blocks of tufa, dating to the middle of the 2nd century B.C. A door which is now walled up led into the other rooms of the prison called « latomia » because they were adapted from the tufa quarries. A circular opening in the pavement of this room was originally the only entrance to an underground chamber where those condemned to death and enemies of the State were tortured and killed, generally by strangulation. This room was circular except on the east side and built in blocks of *peperino*. We know of its sinister fame as a site of death in the midst of darkness and stench from the sources. Those killed here included the followers of Gaius Gracchus and of Cataline, Jugurtha king of Mauritania, Vercingetorix chief of the Arverni, Sejanus prefect of the praetorium of Tiberius. It only appears to be a later legend that St. Peter was kept prisoner here.

Opposite, above: the interior of the Mamertine Prisons and, below, the Arch of Janus. Above: the Forum Boarium.

THE ARCH OF JANUS

A large four-sided marble arch, which stands between the Velabrum and the Forum Boarium, can be identified with an « *arcus divi Constantini* » mentioned in the Regionaries of the Constantinian period, in Region XI. Fragments of the dedicatory inscription from the arch are walled in the facade and interior of the Church of S. Giorgio in Velabro and seem to indicate that it was erected in honor of Constantine, probably by Constantius II around A.D. 256 when he visited Rome.

The conventional name of Arch of Janus derives from the term *Ianus* (patron god of gateways) used to designate covered passageways, arcades and arches.

It measures 12 meters per side and is 16 meters high. The four piers, faced with marble slabs (in part reused), stand on molded plinths. Above the plinth, the two outer faces of each pier have two rows of semi-circular niches with shell-shaped conchas, which held statues and were separated by a cornice. Originally they must have been framed by small columns which in the lower row rested on the cornice of the plinth, and in the upper row rested on the cornice at the height of the opening. The round arches lead into barrel vaults which at their crossing form a cross vault with brick ribbing. The attic, of brick faced with marble, was torn down in 1827 as a medieval addi-

tion. The predilection for a facade of niches framed by small columns on corbels is typical of the 4th century. The Arch of Janus therefore can be compared with the north apse of the Basilica of Maxentius, Maxentius' restructuration in 307 of the temple of Venus in Rome, with the facade of Diocletian's palace in Spalato and with the changes made by Diocletian inside the Curia.

THE FORUM BOARIUM

The so-called Forum Boarium constitutes most of the plain between the Tiber and the group of hills nearest the river (Capitoline, Palatine and Aventine). The area was of enormous importance in the founding of the city of Rome; in fact this was where the two principal trade routes in ancient central Italy crossed: the river Tiber which was at the time navigable, and the north-south route from Etruria to Campania. There was an easy ford downstream from the Isola Tiberina at the spot where Rome's first bridge, the Pons Sublicium, was built. The city's first trading port (*Portus Tiberinus*) was installed in the bend of the river between the Forum Boarium (animal market) and the Forum Holitorium (legume and vegetable market).

The ancient monuments still visible in this area include two exceptionally well-preserved temples which lie fairly

close together in what is now the Piazza Bocca della Verità, corresponding to the old Forum Boarium. The first is known as the **Temple of Fortuna Virilis** but should instead be identified as the Temple of Portunus, an ancient tutelary deity of the port. The building stood very close to the Portus Tiberinus, just outside the Porta Flumentana, and may have been built as early as the period of the kings. It was obviously restored more than once and the present aspect dates to a restoration of the 1st century B.C. The temple stands on a podium in rubblework faced with slabs of travertine. The temple is Ionic pseudoperipteral with four columns on the facade and with the long sides comprised of two columns and five engaged columns on the wall of the cella. The walls of the building are built completely of Aniene tufa. The columns, the bases and the capitals of the engaged columns are in travertine. The entire structure was stuccoed. The original cornice which still preserves the lion protomes is exceptional.

The second temple is the circular structure erroneously indicated as the **Temple of Vesta**. It was, instead, as proved by the discovery of a block inscribed with topographical data, the Temple of Hercules Victor, mentioned in the sources. The building was founded at the end of the 2nd century B.C. by a Roman merchant who had made his fortune in oil. He dedicated the temple to the patron god of the corporation of the *olearii* (Hercules) and had it built near the trading port. The temple is a round peripteral building with twenty Corinthian columns, standing on a stepped crepidoma. The circular cella had an opening on the east. The entablature has been completely lost. The entire building was constructed in Pentelic marble, probably by the Greek architect Hermodoros of Salamina, who had various commissions in Rome in the second half of the 2nd century B.C. The cult statue of the god, called *Hercules Olivarius*, was also by a Greek sculptor, Scopas Minor. As it is now, the building also includes a considerable amount of restoration of the Tiberian age, which involved nine columns and eleven capitals which were remade in luna marble.

Opposite, above: the Temple of Fortuna Virilis and, below, the so-called Temple of Vesta.
Above: the propylaeum of the Portico of Octavia.

PORTICO OF OCTAVIA

The site of the portico is in the Campus Martius, north of the Theater of Marcellus and the Circus Flaminius (of which nothing remains today).

The complex, built by Augustus between 33 and 28 B.C. and dedicated to his sister Octavia, stands on the site of the Porticus Metelli. The first portico had been built by Quintus Caecilius Metellus Macedonicus between 146 and 131 B.C. in honor of his victory in the Macedonian revolt and enclosed the Temple of Juno Regina, built in 179 B.C. by M. Aemilius Lepidus, and the Temple of Jupiter Stator which was set next to it at this time, the first temple in Rome built entirely of marble, by the Greek architect Hermodorus of Salamina.

The Portico of Octavia was destroyed by the fire of A.D. 80 and restored by Domitian. A second reconstruction was undertaken by Septimius Severus after another fire in A.D. 191. The extant remains are of this latter date but the ground plan is provided by the Forma Urbis of Severan date. The building is rectangular in plan and measures 119x132 meters and it had porticoes of two rows of columns on the long sides and two entrance propylaea at the center of a colonnade on the short sides. Inside were the temples of Jupiter Stator and Juno Regina, the former a *peripteros sine postico*, that is with colonnades on three sides and engaged columns on the back, the second prostyle with six columns on the front and three at the sides. Augustus also had the Curia Octaviae built in the portico, an apsed building that lay behind the two temples, and the Greek and Latin libraries.

The Portico of Octavia was also a real museum and the works exhibited included 34 equestrian statues in bronze by Lysippus, taken from a sanctuary in Macedon and representing Alexander the Great with his horsemen at the battle of Granicus, and a bronze statue of Cornelia, the mother of the Gracchi, of which the base remains. Parts of the complex that are still visible and in good condition include the propylaeum on the south side, which projected inwards and outwards with two facades consisting of four Corinthian columns topped by pediments, with an inscription on the architrave celebrating the Severan restoration. Two columns of the external facade are still standing while the other two were replaced in the Middle Ages by an arch.

Above: the remains of the Theater of Marcellus near the columns of the Temple of Apollo Sosianus.
Opposite, above: a reconstruction of the area of the Theater of Marcellus and the Temple of Apollo with the Tiber, at the center of which is the Tiberine Island.
Below: a detail of the Theater of Marcellus as it once was.

THEATER OF MARCELLUS

The project for the so-called Theater of Marcellus dates to Caesar's time, but the building was finished in 13 B.C. by Augustus who officially dedicated it in the name of his nephew Marcellus, his first designated heir, who died early in 23 B.C.

In Rome the theatrical representations (*ludi scaenici*), so important in the election campaigns, were traditionally held in a provvisory wooden theater, near the old Temple of Apollo in the Campus Martius. Not until 55 B.C. did Pompey build the city's first masonry theater. The building planned by Caesar was on the same site as the provvisory theater. The installation of the large *cavea* destroyed a part of the curved side of the Circus Flaminius (erected in 221 B.C.) and two small temples, rebuilt in the large exedra behind the scaena. In 17 B.C., although the work was not yet finished, Augustus had the famous *ludi saeculares*, sung by Horace, celebrated in the theater. In the 13th century the building was occupied by the noble Savelli family; in the 18th century it passed to the Orsini. The fine Renaissance palace that occupies the third floor

of the exterior facade of the cavea is the work of the architect Baldassarre Peruzzi.

The theater must have been built on powerful substructures, and the front was provided with a facade of 41 arches, framed by engaged columns, on three floors. The first two floors are Doric and Ionic orders, the third, of which nothing remains, must have been an attic closed by Corinthian pilasters. It was originally 32.60 m. high. The interior ambulatory and the radial walls of the cunei (wedge-shaped sectors of seats) are in *opus quadratum* of tufa for the first 10 meters down, in *opus caementicium* with a facing of *opus reticulatum* in the inner part. It has been calculated that the *cavea* (diam. 129.80 m.) could hold between 15 and 20,000 spectators, making it the largest theater in Rome as far as audience capacity was concerned. Beyond the orchestra (diam. m. 37) was the stage, of which nothing remains. On either side were apsed halls, of which a pier and a column of one are still standing. Behind the stage was a large semi-circular exedra with two small temples. The building was also noticeable for its rich decoration, still visible in the Doric frieze on the lower order.

ISOLA TIBERINA

According to an old written tradition, the small island in the Tiber now known as Isola Tiberina was formed when the grain that had been harvested in the Campus Martius (private property of the Tarquins) was thrown into the river after the expulsion of the Etruscan kings from Rome. Naturally this is only legend; actually the island has a geological formation like that of the hill nearest the river (the Capitoline) and its core is comprised of magmatic rock on which considerable amounts of fluvial detritus have been deposited.

No one knows when the island was occupied for the first time. In any case its location played a determining role in the foundation of the city. In fact, since the islet divides the course of the Tiber in two in the proximity of one of its bends, it served as an easy means of communication from one bank of the river to the other. The first bridge in Rome, the Pons Sublicium (from *sublicae* = wooden pier), was built by king Ancus Marcius somewhat downstream from the Isola Tiberina where an important ford

in the communications system of central Italy already existed.

The first important building erected on the island dates to 291 B.C. This was the Temple of Aesculapius. Written sources refer that in 293 B.C. a disastrous plague struck the city of Rome. In keeping with tradition the Sibylline texts were consulted. These sacred prophetic texts used in case of dire need ordered the Romans to send an embassy to Epidauros, site of the cult of Aesculapius, the Greek god of medicine. Thus the trireme Rome sent to Greece between 291 and 289 B.C. returned with no less than the sacred serpent, the symbol of the god. When the ship docked at Navalia, the military port on the banks of the Campus Martius, the snake escaped and flinging itself into the river swam to the Isola Tiberina where it disappeared, thus indicating the precise spot where the new temple was to rise. Nothing remains today of the original building, but the site is probably that of the 17th-century Church of S. Bartolomeo, and the well that still exists near the altar could correspond to the sacred fount. The porticoes of the sanctuary of Aesculapius were a real hospital. Numerous inscriptions preserved mention miraculous healings or dedications to the god. In the Middle Ages the island continued to be set aside as a hospital, thanks in part to its being isolated from the inhabited areas, and it is still used as such with the Hospital of the Fatebenefratelli, adjacent to the small Church of S. Giovanni Calibita.

In antiquity the island was also joined to the city by two bridges. The one which still today connects it to the left bank, near the Theater of Marcellus, is the ancient Pons Fabricius. It was built in 62 B.C. and may or may not have been preceded by another bridge or a ferry. A large inscription, set above the arches and repeated both on the upstream side as well as the downstream side, bears the name of the builder: Lucius Fabricius, son of Caius, *curator viarum*, (a magistrate charged with the urban traffic). On the arcade nearest to the bank of Campus Martius is another later inscription with the names of the consuls of 21 B.C.; they must have restored the bridge which was damaged in the terrible flood of 23 B.C., which completely destroyed the old Pons Sublicius. The Pons Fabricius is 62 m. long and 5.50 m. wide; the two large slightly flattened arches have a span of 24.50 m. and spring from a massive central pier, which is pierced by a small arch that serves to relieve the pressure of the

Opposite: the Tiberine Island as it is today and, below, a reconstruction with, in the background, the Temple of Aesculapius.

99

Above and opposite: two views of the Tiberine Island as it is today.

Opposite: a reconstruction of the Tiberine Island in the bend of the Tiber in front of the Theater of Marcellus.

water on the structure during floods. Originally it was built in blocks of tufa and *peperino* faced with slabs of travertine, only some of which are still extant; the brick revestment was added under Pope Innocent XI (1679). At the beginning of the bridge near the Campus Martius, two four-sided herms have survived. They supported the original railing, in bronze.

The other bridge which joins the island to Trastevere is no longer the original one. The Pons Cestius was torn down between 1888 and 1892. It had been built in the first century B.C., perhaps by the praetor of 44 B.C., the same C. Cestius to whom the famous funeral monument in the shape of a pyramid is dedicated. In A.D. 370 it was

restored by the emperor Valentinian I.

The unique form of the Isola Tiberina in the shape of an elongated boat, together with the remembrance of the ship which had brought the serpent of Aesculapius to Rome, gave rise to an odd architectural adaptation of the site which probably dates to the first century. The easternmost point of the island was turned into the prow of a trireme, built in *peperino* and faced with blocks of travertine. Still in their places are a bust of Aesculapius with the serpent twined around his wand and a bull-head shaped element which reproduces the hitching point for the mooring hawser. The westernmost point was also structured in the form of a stern but nothing is left.

PANTHEON

Of all the buildings of ancient Rome the Pantheon is the best preserved thanks to the fact that the Byzantine emperor Phocas donated it to Pope Boniface IV and that it was then transformed into a church as S. Maria ad Martyres (A.D. 609).

The first building was erected in 27 B.C. by Marcus Vipsanius Agrippa, the faithful advisor of Augustus, as part of the general restructuring of the central area of the Campus Martius, which had just then become his property. The temple was conceived for the glorification of the *gens Iulia* and called Pantheon (*sanctissimum*): all the planetary divinities in addition to Mars and Venus, the protectors of Augustus' family, may have been honored here. Agrippa's building, as results from excavations carried out at the end of the 19th century, was rectangular (m. 19.82x43.76) and oriented south, not north as it is now. The facade was on the long side, preceded by a pronaos, and in front of it was an open circular area, paved in travertine. This temple was damaged in the fire of A.D. 80 and was restored by Domitian. After another fire in Trajan's time, the temple was completely rebuilt by Hadrian, between 118 and 128, in the form we still see today. This fact is confirmed by information furnished by a Latin historian and by the factory marks on the

bricks, which bear the consular dates. The inscription on the frieze of the porch, *M(arcus) Agrippa L(uci) f(ilius) co(n)s(ul) tertium fecit*, was therefore placed there by Hadrian who never put his own name on any of the monuments he built.

Hadrian's reconstruction profoundly modified the original building. The facade was set facing north, the porch was set on the site occupied by the original temple, and the large rotunda coincided with the open area in front. Still today, the large columned porch has a facade composed of eight columns in grey granite. Two red granite columns each are set behind the first, third, sixth, and eighth column of the facade, thus forming three aisles. The central aisle, which is the widest, leads to the entrance. The side aisles end in two large niches destined for the statues of Agrippa and Augustus. The tympanum was decorated with a crowned eagle in bronze of which only the fix-holes still remain. The ceiling of the porch was also decorated in bronze but this was removed by Pope Urban VIII Barberini (which lies at the root of the famous pasquinade: « *quod non fecerunt barbari, fecerunt Barberini* »).

Behind the porch is a massive construction in brick, which joins it to the Rotonda, a gigantic cylinder with a wall that is six meters thick, divided into three superposed sectors, marked externally by cornices. The wall gets

Opposite: the imposing facade of the
Pantheon with its tympanum, perfectly
maintained throughout the centuries, as
shown by the reconstruction above.

Right: a reconstruction of the Pantheon
as it looked in antiquity in which the vast
dome is seen to its best advantage.
Above, to the left of the building, are the
Saepta Julia.

lighter as it rises, and the thickness of the walls, with brick vaulting in various places, is not always completely solid. The height of the Rotonda to the top of the dome is precisely that of its diameter (m. 43.30) so that the interior space is a perfect sphere. The dome is a masterpiece of engineering: it is the largest dome ever covered by masonry and was cast in a single operation on an imposing wooden centering.

The interior of the building has six distyle niches at the sides and a semicircular exedra at the back, with eight small aedicules in between which have alternating arched and triangular pediments. The dome is decorated with five tiers of lacunar coffering except for a smooth band near the oculus, the circular opening (9 m. diam.) which illuminates the interior.

CASTEL S. ANGELO

Castel S. Angelo, whose imposing mass still dominates the panorama of Rome, and which is known as the Mole Adriana, was not originally built for defensive purposes but as the funeral monument of the emperors. Up to Nerva, the final resting place of the ashes of the emperors was the Mausoleum of Augustus, built in the northernmost part of the Campus Martius. Trajan's remains, in the absence of space in the imperial sepulcher, were placed in the base of the historied column raised in his enormous forum. Hadrian then had work begun on a new mausoleum, destined to become the dynastic sepulcher of the Antonines: in fact all the members of the imperial family from Hadrian himself up to Caracalla were buried there.

The site chosen for the new building was in the area of the Vatican, still relatively free of buildings, crossed by important roads lined with tombs, and mostly occupied by private villas, the finest of which ended up as imperial property. Hadrian's Mausoleum was built on one of these lots of land, the so-called Horti of Domizia, on the right banks of the Tiber, right across from the Campus Martius. A new bridge (called Pons Aelius from the *nomen* of the emperor) which still exists as Ponte S. Angelo was built to put the monument in communication with the Campus Martius. This bridge flanked Nero's Bridge, further downstream. It consisted of three large central arches and two inclined ramps supported by three smaller arches on the right bank and two on the left bank. The bridge served principally to connect the *ustrinum*, the monumental platform on which Hadrian and his wife Sabina were to be cremated, erected in the Campus Martius, with the tomb on the other side of the Tiber.

Most of the structural parts of the mausoleum, which was

Above: a view of the interior and of the coffered vault of the Pantheon. Left: the Aurelian Column.

Opposite, above: Castel Sant'Angelo as it is today and, below, as it looked when it was a mausoleum for the Antonines.

Above: the front of Castel Sant'Angelo seen from the bridge before it. In the overleaf: the Ara Pacis.

incorporated into Castel S. Angelo in the Middle Ages, have been preserved. The building consisted of an enormous quadrangular basement, 89 m. per side and 15 m. high. It was built in *opus latericium* with radiating chambers covered with vaulting. On top was a cylindrical drum (diam. 64 m., height 21 m.) flanked by radial walls. A tumulus of earth planted with trees rose up over the drum with its massive core in *peperino* (grey lithoid tufa) and *opus caementicium*. Along the edges were decorative marble statues and at the center, raised even higher up, was a podium with columns, on top of which was a bronze quadriga with the statue of Hadrian. The exterior of the enclosure was faced with Luna marble and with inscriptions of the *tituli* of the personages buried in the monument; engaged pilasters were set at the corners and the upper part was decorated with a frieze of garlands and bucrania (fragments are preserved in the Museo del Castello). The drum was faced on the outside with travertine and fluted pilaster strips. The entire monument was enclosed in a wall with bronze gates, decorated with peacocks (two are in the Vatican), perhaps a funerary symbol.

The original entrance to the tomb, with three openings, was on the side of the base that faces the river. The cur-

rent entrance is at least three meters higher up. From here a corridor (*dromos*) led to a square vestibule with a semicircular alcove on the back wall, faced with yellow Numidian marble. The helicoidal gallery which rises ten meters and leads to the funeral chamber begins to the right of the vestibule. The vault of this corridor, with four vertical light wells, is in rubblework; the pavement still retains traces of its original mosaic decoration while the walls were covered with marble to a height of three meters. The funeral chamber, right at the center of the massive drum, is square (3 m. per side) with three rectangular niches; illumination is from two oblique windows in the vault. The cinerary urns of the emperors were placed in this room. Above the funerary chamber were two superposed cellae which by means of an annular corridor led to the top of the monument.

As early as A.D. 403 the emperor Honorius may have incorporated the building in an outpost bastion of the Aurelian Walls. In 537, when it was already a fortress, it was attacked by Vitiges and his Goths. In the 10th century it was transformed into a castle and its present name derives from a popular belief in the apparition of the Archangel Michael on its summit, which dates back to the Middle Ages.

ARA PACIS

Contemporary literary and epigraphic sources provide ample information as to the foundation date and the reasons which lay behind the erection of this extremely important monument of Roman art. The *Res Gestae Divi Augusti*, the emperor's official autobiography, and the *Fasti* of Ovid inform us that the Roman Senate voted an altar to the *Pax Augusta* in the Campus Martius to commemorate the return of Augustus from Spain and Gaul, celebrating the new policies of Rome and the beginning of what they hoped was a period of peace. The altar was begun in 13 B.C. on July 4th, near the Via Flaminia on property belonging to Agrippa, the general of Augustus who had become a member of the imperial family after his marriage to Julia, the emperor's daughter. The *dedicatio*, that is the inauguration upon completion of the work, was celebrated on January 30, in 9 B.C.

The discovery of the Ara Pacis dates to 1568, when nine of its sculptured blocks were found under the Renaissance Palazzo Peretti (now Almagià). In 1879 Von Duhn identified these marble fragments for the first time as being remains of the famous monument. Systematic excavations were undertaken in 1903 with the discovery of the architectural parts of the altar. Finally in 1937-38, for the Augustan bi-milennial, the excavations were terminated and the altar was reconstructed in a pavilion built for this purpose next to the Mausoleum of Augustus, near the Tiber. At present, therefore, the Ara Pacis no longer occupies its original site and its orientation has also been changed from east-west to north-south. The monument is composed of a rectangular marble enclosure on a podium (m. 11.65x10.62) access to which was via a staircase, with two large doors (3.60 m. wide), that opened on the long sides which originally faced on the Via Flaminia and on the Campus Martius. The actual altar was inside the enclosure. It is set on a three-stepped podium and, on the west, five other steps permitted the priest to reach the top of the altar on which the sacrificial rites took place.

The entire enclosure, both inside and out, is covered with a rich sculptural decoration. On the outside it is subdivided into two distinct sections: at the top, a figured frieze; below a frieze with ornamental acanthus scroll motifs. The two sections are separated by a meander band. These divisions are framed by pilaster strips, four at the corners and two near the doors, decorated with candelabra of vegetable motifs, which support the entablature (completely rebuilt) which must have been crowned by acroteria.

The panels with mythical-allegorical scenes are on the longer sides of the enclosure, next to the doors. The two panels on the west side contain scenes of the sacrifice of Aeneas to the Penates (on the right) and the Lupercal (on the left), the grotto where the legendary wolf nursed the twins Remus and Romulus. The first scene is well preserved: Aeneas *velato capite* and with the *sceptrum* in his left hand, is shown as he sacrifices the white sow with

A detail of the figured frieze which decorates the exterior of the Ara Pacis. Opposite, above: the Mausoleum of Augustus as it is today and, below, a reconstruction.

her 30 piglets to the Penates of Lavinium, who are represented by a small temple, above left.

The second scene has been almost entirely lost. All that remains is the shepherd Faustulus on the right and the god Mars on the left, as well as fragments of water plants which represent the banks of the Tiber.

The two panels on the east side contain, to the right, a fragment with the representation of Rome dressed as an Amazon, while on the left is the panel, which is almost complete, known as Saturnia Tellus (the personification of Italia). At the center sits a blooming female figure with two children in her lap, and a semi-nude nymph on either side, the one on the right on a marine monster, the one on the left flying on a swan, who symbolize the other elements (water and air). The landscape is also clearly indicated: to the right the ocean, at the center the earth and rocks populated by domestic animals and flowering plants, to the left the rivers represented by reeds and a pitcher from which water is flowing. The scene is an allegory of Peace, which, thanks to Augustus, brings prosperity back to Italy, enriching it with bountiful crops and herds.

The short sides contain the representation of a sacrificial procession, unified but organized into two distinct groups: one with the priests and those assigned to the cult, and one with all the members of the imperial family. The composition is closely bound to motives of protocol: in the first group the conventional figures of priests and magistrates are arranged hierarchically according to their offices (*ordo sacerdotorum*); in the second, the members of the emperor's family, more clearly characterized, are arranged in order of their succession to the throne, which Augustus conceived during the years in which the monument was being built.

The interior of the enclosure probably reproduces in marble the temporary wooden fence (*templum*) erected for the ceremony of 13 B.C. when the altar was vowed (*constitutio*). At the bottom is the vertical lath fence; above, a motif of garlands with patera and bucrania, which must have been hung on it. The sides of the altar inside the enclosure have been preserved, decorated with tendrils and resting on winged lions. A small low relief frieze runs all around the *mensa* (table), inside and outside; it represents the annual sacrifice performed on the altar.

MAUSOLEUM OF AUGUSTUS

Augustus' imposing funeral monument today stands alone in the middle of the vast Piazza Augusto Imperatore. This square was the result of Fascist town planning. Between 1936 and 1938, for the bi-millenial celebrations for Augustus, all the buildings of the old quarter which surrounded it were demolished to free the remains of the monument. A pavilion was also built along one side for the reconstruction of the Ara Pacis.

The dynastic tomb of the first emperor of Rome is a circular structure (87 m. in diameter) consisting of a series of concentric walls in tufa connected by radiating walls. The outer wall faced with travertine (12 m. high) may have been decorated at the top with a Doric frieze with triglyphs and metopes. Behind it is the enormously thick wall (circa 14 m.) in *opus caementicium*, lightened by semicircular niches filled in with earth; further in, two rows of concentric walls, joined together by radiating arms of walling, create a second series of inaccessible chambers. The first accessible chamber lies at the end of the long entrance corridor (*dromos*) which cuts through the structures described above. This room is a sector of a circle and is circumscribed by a large circular wall faced in travertine. Two entrances in this wall lead to the annular corridor which rings the cella. This imposing wall provided the substructure for a drum, which must have emerged from the tumulus itself, probably as a base for a funerary temple that no longer exists. The cella is circu-

lar with an entrance on its axis and three niches placed radially. At the center is a pier inside which is a square chamber. The tomb of Augustus was here, in corrispondence to the bronze statue of the emperor which was at the top of the pier. The three niches of the cella contained other tombs of important member of the Julio-Claudian dynasty. Two Egyptian obelisks stood before the door of the building which opened to the south. Two piers on either side of the entrance held the bronze tablets with the official autobiography of Augustus (*Res Gestae Divi Augusti*), a copy of which is to be seen on the side of the pavilion which houses the Ara Pacis.

Below: the Baths of Diocletian as they originally were and, opposite, as they are today.

THE BATHS OF DIOCLETIAN

The Baths of Diocletian are the largest thermae ever built in Rome. They went up in a relatively brief period of time, between A.D. 298 and 306 under the two Augustan tetrarchs Diocletian and Maximianus, as witnessed by the dedicatory inscription. The establishment was built in one of the most densely populated zones of Rome, between the hills of the Esquiline, Quirinal and Viminal. A special deviation of the old Aqua Marcia aqueduct supplied water for the enormous cistern (91 m. long) which was demolished once and for all in 1876. Reference to these baths is still to be found in the name « Termini » by which the nearby railroad station is now known. The structures of the original complex of buildings have been greatly modified by later superstructures and variations in the fabric of the surrounding streets but they are in part still legible. The total area occupied measured 380 by 370 meters. The main bath building was at the center of a rectangular enclosure with a large semi-circular exedra on one of the long sides (corresponding to what is now the Piazza della Republica), two rotundas at the corners and numerous hemicycles along the perimeter. The plan of the main building is along the lines of the great imperial baths: a large central basilica, the *calidarium-tepidarium-natatio* complex arranged on a median axis along the short side, with palaestrae and accessory services balancing each other on either side of the axis.

The entire structure is built in *opus latericium*, or brick. It is calculated that about 3000 people could use the establishment at one time. The *calidarium* (hot bath) was rectangular with four semicircular alcoves; one of these is now the entrance to the Church of S. Maria degli Angeli into which Michelangelo (1566) converted the central principal hall. In spite of the modifications, in which Vanvitelli (1749) also had a hand, it still retains its original aspect. The church occupies two side chambers as well as the central hall. The apses on the northeast side then covered part of the *natatio* (swimming pool); the small circular room with two square exedrae, which serves as a porch, was the *tepidarium* (warm bath). Another part of the original building is now included in the Museo Nazionale Romano, installed in the ex-convent of the Carthusians which was built in the midst of the ruins of the baths.

A view of the zone of the Quirinal, rebuilt in the model of ancient Rome in the Museo della Civiltà Romana. The large Temple of Serapis, with the Baths of Constantine before it, rises up in the center.

A detail of the model of ancient Rome reproducing the area of the Column of Marcus Aurelius (at the center), near which are the Temple of Hadrian and the Temple of Matidia (above).

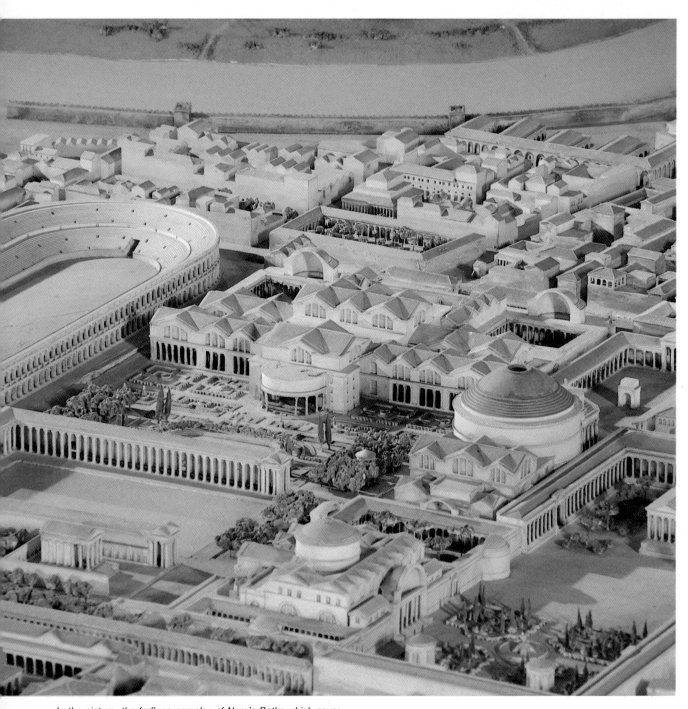

In the picture, the farflung complex of Nero's Baths which cover the area between the Pantheon and the Stadium of Domitian as they looked 2000 years ago.

The Theater and the cryptoporticus known as « crypta Balbi » with, on the left, the Porticus Minucia Frumentari and, on the right, the Porticus Philippi.

Opposite, two views of what remains of the Baths of Caracalla and, above, the reconstruction of the enormous complex with, below, the Via Ardeatina and the Aurelian Walls.

BATHS OF CARACALLA

The Baths of Caracalla are the most imposing and best preserved example of thermae from the Imperial period still extant. They were built by Caracalla beginning in A.D. 212. The site chosen was a small valley between the slopes of the so-called Piccolo Aventino and the Via Nova, where an artificial basin, called « Piscina Publica », may already have existed. A special branch of the old Aqua Marcia aqueduct was provided to bring water to the new baths. Work continued until 216, at which point it was dedicated. The baths contined to function until 537 when, during the siege of Vitiges and his Goths, the aqueducts of the city were cut.

In the 16th century, excavations carried out in the enormous building brought to light various works of art including the Farnese Bull and the Hercules, now in the National Museum of Naples. Mosaics with athletes, which decorated the hemicycles of the large side courtyards of the thermae, were discovered in 1824 (Vatican Museums). In their ground plan the Baths of Caracalla clearly distin-guished between the actual bath sector and the surround-ings where all the accessory non-bathing services were located. This enclosure, which measured 337x328 meters, consisted of a portico; on the north-east where the monumental entrance was set, it was preceded by a series of concamerations on two levels, which supported the immense artificial earthwork on which the baths were built. Two imposing exedrae still stand on either side of the enclosure. Each one has three rooms: a central room with an apse, preceded by a colonnade, and flanked by a rectangular chamber on one side and an interesting octagonal nymphaeum, covered with a dome on pendentives, on the other. At the back of the enclosure was a flattened exedra, like a stadium with one side missing, with tiers from which to watch gymnastic competitions. The enormous cisterns lay below, arranged on two levels and with a capacity of 80,000 liters of water. Two apsed rooms, one on either side of the exedra, were libraries. A colonnaded walkway, of which almost nothing remains, ran along the inner side of the enclosure. It was probably raised.

The building in the center, shifted towards the main en-

117

Above: a two-colored mosaic pavement with dolphins inside the Baths of Caracalla. Opposite, a portion of the remains of the baths.

trance and separated from the enclosure by a vast garden, was the actual bathing establishment. Access was through four doors on the northeast facade. Two of these led to vestibules adjacent to the *natatio* (swimming pool), and the other two opened onto rooms which led to the palaestrae. At present, entrance is through the second door from the right and the itinerary is quite like that followed in antiquity by the bathers. The vestibule leads on the right into a square chamber, flanked by two small rooms on either side, covered with barrel vaults. This was the *apodyterium* (dressing-room). Next came one of the two large palaestrae, set symmetrically along the short sides of the building. They consisted of large peristyles (m. 50x20) with columns in Numidian yellow on three sides; a vast hemicycle opened off one side of the portico through six columns, while the other side, without a portico, had five rooms, the one in the center with an apse. This is where the bathing itinerary generally started after various sports and exercises had been done in the palaestra. From here the itinerary led to a series of variously shaped smaller and larger rooms with tubs for special

baths and oiling (*unctuaria*). An elliptical chamber covered with a cross vault and with small oblique entrances meant to preserve the heat as much as possible was a *laconicum* (turkish bath). After this came the imposing *calidarium* (hot bath): an enormous circular room (35 m. diam.) covered by a dome supported on eight piers and illuminated by two rows of large windows in the drum. After the *calidarium* came the *tepidarium* (temperate bath), a more modest rectangular chamber flanked by two pools. Next came the large central hall, the *frigidarium*. It was a large basilica, 58x24 m., covered with three large cross vaults, which were supported on eight piers against which stood eight granite columns. One of these remained in place until 1563 when it was transported to Florence and set up in Piazza S. Trinita. On either side the hall was a rectangular room, in the center of which were the two granite basins now in the Piazza Farnese. The *natatio*, which could also be reached from the *frigidarium*, was uncovered. It has a fine front elevation with groups of niches between columns, once meant to contain statues.

Above: a stretch of the Aurelian Walls. Opposite: the Porta Appia (now Porta San Sebastiano).

AURELIAN WALLS

Literary tradition attributes the earliest walls of the city of Rome to king Servius Tullius, which would date them to the middle of the 6th century B.C. Scholars however do not yet agree as to whether this archaic circle of walls existed. The presence of various stretches of wall built in *cappellaccio* (a particular type of local tufa), still to be seen in certain parts of the city, seem however to confirm the traditional date. After the Gauls occupied the city (390 B.C.) a more substantial wall was built in the so-called tufa of Grotta Oscura from quarries that had become accessible after the conquest of Veio (396 B.C.). The building technique used was that known from sources as *saxum quadratum* in which the rows of ashlars, each about 59 cm. high, are laid alternatively leaders and stretchers without using any mortar. The wall was almost eleven kilometers long and around ten meters high while it was more than four meters thick. These walls constituted Rome's defense throughout the late republican period and for a good part of the Imperial period. They were obviously frequently restored in the course of the centuries.

The need to enlarge the city walls was not felt until the 3rd century A.D., both because the inhabited quarters had gone way beyond the perimeter of the old walls and because the barbarians had for some time already been a threat to the Empire and the capital ran the risk of their arrival, as had happened with Athens which was sacked in A.D. 270 by the Heruli. The emperor Aurelian, involved in campaigns ever further away (especially against Zenobia, Queen of Palymra), decided to provide the Urbs with a new set of city walls. Work began in 271 and advanced rapidly so that the essential parts had already been completed when Aurelian died in 275. The undertaking was then finished by Probus. The walls, built primarily by the urban guilds of masons, initally constituted a modest but unified defensive system, which sufficed in halting the incursions of peoples who where technically unprepared to undertake long sieges. The entire work is in *opus latericium*, in other works a brick curtain wall, which was six meters high and 3,50 meters thick. Every one hundred Roman feet (m. 29.60) it was provided with a square tower that had an upper chamber for *ballistae*. The principal gates consisted of two covered arched entrances faced in travertine, and framed by two semicircular towers. The more modest gates were simply inserted at the center of a stretch of wall between two square towers. The allover perimeter of the fortification measures around nineteen kilometers. It follows a strategic route which includes the hills and large urban structures within its perimeter. A surprising number of prece-

dent buildings were encompassed in the city walls, a sign of the haste with which the work proceeded. It has been calculated that about one tenth of the walls is comprised of pre-existing buildings.

In the time of Maxentius (306-312) the fortification was already in need of restoration, recognizable from the technique used, the *opus vittatum*, a facing which consisted of horizontal bands of tufa alternated with tufa ashlars. But it was under Honorius (401-402) that the more consistent work was done in preparation for attacks by the Goths. The height of the wall was doubled, the precedent sentinel walk was replaced with a covered gallery with numerous slits and above this a new crenellated sentry walk was built. The double entrances of the gates were reduced to one and they were furnished with counter doors on the inside. The semicircular towers became higher and the aspect was that of small self-sufficient fortresses. It was at this time that Hadrian's Mausoleum was included in the walls as an outpost castle on the right bank of the Tiber.

The Aurelian walls begin north of the Porta Flaminia (what is now Porta del Popolo) and continue (clockwise) along the Viale del Muro Torto, including the Pincio, as far as the Salaria and the Nomentana Gates. Here the

Castra Praetoria, the praetorian encampment built by Tiberius, was enclosed in the fortifications. Various gates opened on the east side, including the Tiburtina, which made use of a precedent monumental passageway built under Augustus, and the double gate known as Maggiore, which encloses two arches of the Claudian aqueduct. The wall then makes a sharp turn southwestwards, to include various structures (among which an amphitheater) of the Domus Sessoriana, an imperial villa built in the Severan dynasty.

The best preserved part of the wall is the southern part, which embraces the last outcrops of the Caelian Hill as far as the Porta Ardeatina. One section that runs between the Porta S. Sebastiano (ancient Porta Appia), the best preserved in the wall, and the Sangallo Bastion, is also open to the public for walks inside. Still further on is the fine Porta *Ostiensis*.

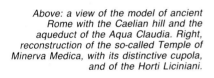

Above: a view of the model of ancient Rome with the Caelian hill and the aqueduct of the Aqua Claudia. Right, reconstruction of the so-called Temple of Minerva Medica, with its distinctive cupola, and of the Horti Liciniani.

A reconstruction with, to the left of the Tiber, the district around the Via Portuense and the Porta Portuensis. Right: the Emporium, the Porticus Aemilia and, on the far right, the grain storehouses Horrea Galbana. Opposite, above: the Pyramid of Cestius and the Porta San Paolo as they are now and, below, a reconstruction of the two monuments.

PORTA S. PAOLO AND THE PYRAMID OF C. CESTIUS

What is now known as **Porta S. Paolo** is one of the best preserved city gates (the other is the Porta S. Sebastiano) in the imposing circle of the Aurelian Walls. Its original name was Porta Ostiensis and as usual this was derived from the name of the road which started at the gate. Despite this, the oldest route followed by the Via Ostiense, the road that led to the great seaport of Rome, ran through a postern south of the Pyramid of Cestius, which was already closed in the time of Maxentius. The current name of the gate derives from the large early Christian Basilica of S. Paolo fuori le Mura, about two kilometers away. Originally the gate had two entrances framed by semicircular towers. Under Maxentius (A.D. 306-312), two pincer walls with a counter gate were added, also with two passageways in travertine. Under Honorius (395-423), the two passageways of the main entrance became one and the towers were raised. It was through this gate that Totila's Goths entered Rome in 544 during the Gotho-Byzantine war. The rooms inside the building now house the Museo della via Ostiense. A curious funeral monument of the early Imperial period, the **Pyramid of C. Cestius**, was set next to the Porta Ostiensis during the construction of the Aurelian walls. The building was obviously inspired by Egyptian models, of the Ptolemaic rather than Pharaonic period, fashionable in Rome after the conquest of Egypt (30 B.C.). The base measures 29.50 m. on each side and the pyramid is 36.40 m. high. The foundations are in *opus caementicium* covered with blocks of travertine while the walls are faced with marble slabs. On the west side is a small door that leads into the funeral chamber. This hollow in the concrete core has a rectangular ground plan (m. 5,85x4) and is covered with a barrel vault and faced with *opus latericium*, a facing of brick. The wall was then plastered and richly painted in the so-called third Pompeian style. Interest has centered on the building ever since the Middle Ages when it was called « Meta Remi ». An inscription placed on the monument records the fact that in 1660 Pope Alexander VII authorized the excavation. Four antique inscriptions, one on the east side, one on the west, and two engraved on the pedestals which supported the bronze statues of the deceased (in the Capitoline Museums), document the public offices and the heirs of the man for whom the tomb was made.

Above: the Canopus inside Hadrian's Villa in Tivoli. Opposite: two stretches of the archaeological zone of Ostia Antica.

TIVOLI

Right outside Rome, Tivoli, the ancient *Tibur*, was already a favorite holiday resort for the Romans as well as a place for the worship of local divinities.

Tivoli is the site of an imposing architectural complex,**Hadrian's Villa**. This emperor's gifts as an architect can be seen in the series of palaces, baths, theaters, etc. which he had built there between 118 and 134, and which were meant to remind him, here in Italy, of the places he most loved in Greece and the Near East.

Bought by the Itaalian government in 1870 from the Braschi family which had owned it since the beginning of the 19th century, the villa was restored, while many of the works of art (especially sculpture) from the site can now be seen in the rooms of the Museo Nazionale Romano. Mention will be made only of some of the best known and important places in the complex. For an idea of the entire set-up (and as orientation) a study of the model at the entrance, even though it is more a matter of hypothesis, can be useful. The monuments include the Stoà Poikile (commonly called Pecile) and the Naval Theater, the Small Thermae and the Great Thermae, the Canopus (with obvious reference to the sanctuary in Egypt), the Museum (with the precious objects found in the excavations, including a copy of the *Amazon* by Phidias), and lastly the Emperor's Palace subdivided into three blocks and aptly described as a « city in the shape of a palace ».

OSTIA ANTICA

The excavations of Ostia Antica contain a great number and variety of remains from the antique Roman city: tombs, mosaics, temples, baths, piazzas and dwellings. These remains are among the most important to be found on the entire archaeological map in Italy. Of particular architectural interest are: the **Baths of Neptune**, precedend by an extensive arcade; the **Baths of the Forum**, dating from the 2nd century A.D.; the splendid **Baths of the Seven Sages**; the little **Round Temple**; the **Temple of the Goddess Ceres** in the Piazzale delle Corporazioni, paved with magnificient mosaics; the **Temple of the Triad** (Capitolium); the **Tablinium** (later the **Caesareum**), place of worship of the emperors; the small and flawless **Theater of Agrippa**, restored and enlarged in part by Septimius Severus and Caracalla; a minute **Sanctuary** dedicated to Jove Sabazio (a divinity of Oriental origin); the picturesque **Tavern of Fortunato**; the **House of Paintings**, with spacious vaulted rooms and large windows; and the **Museo Ostiense** (Museum of Ostia) in which a winding sequence of rooms displays a rich collection of archaelogical finds from the site such as capitals, inscriptions, amphora, and brick seals.

INDEX